P9-AQM-605

Reliability for the Social Sciences

MEASUREMENT METHODS FOR THE SOCIAL SCIENCES SERIES

Measurement Methods for the Social Sciences is a series designed to provide professionals and students in the social sciences and education with succinct and illuminating texts on measurement methodology. Beginning with the foundations of measurement theory and encompassing applications on the cutting edge of social science measurement, each volume is expository, limited in its mathematical demands, and designed for self-study as well as formal instruction. Volumes are richly illustrated; each includes exercises with solutions enabling readers to validate their understanding and confirm their learning.

Titles in this series . . .

1. GENERALIZABILITY THEORY: A PRIMER
   Richard J. Shavelson and Noreen M. Webb
2. FUNDAMENTALS OF ITEM RESPONSE THEORY
   Ronald K. Hambleton, H. Swaminathan, and H. Jane Rogers
3. RELIABILITY FOR THE SOCIAL SCIENCES: Theory and Applications
   Ross E. Traub
4. METHODS FOR IDENTIFYING BIASED TEST ITEMS
   Gregory Camilli and Lorrie A. Shepard

Reliability for the Social Sciences

THEORY AND APPLICATIONS

volume 3

Ross E. Traub

SAGE Publications
International Educational and Professional Publisher
Thousand Oaks   London   New Delhi

For information address:

SAGE Publications, Inc.
2455 Teller Road
Thousand Oaks, California 91320

SAGE Publications Ltd.
6 Bonhill Street
London EC2A 4PU
United Kingdom

SAGE Publications India Pvt. Ltd.
M-32 Market
Greater Kailash I
New Delhi 110 048 India

Printed in the United States of America

Library of Congress Cataloging-in-Publication Data

Traub, Ross E.
    Reliability for the social sciences: theory and applications /
Ross E. Traub.
        p.   cm.—(Measurement methods for the social sciences
series, v. 3)
    Includes bibliographical references and index.
    ISBN 0-8039-4324-5.—ISBN 0-8039-4325-3 (pbk.)
    1. Social sciences—Statistical methods. I. Title. II. Series.
HA29.T668   1994
300'.1'5195—dc20   93-40760
                                                        CIP

94 95 96 97 98 10 9 8 7 6 5 4 3 2 1

Sage Production Editor: Yvonne Könneker

Contents

Series Editor's Introduction ix

Preface xi

1. Introduction 1
   A Word About Measurement 1
   Overview 3
   Exercise 4

2. A Brief Statistical Interlude 5
   Variable 5
   Random Variable 6
   Expected Value of a Random Variable 7
   The Variance of a Random Variable 11
   The Covariance of Two Random Variables 12
   The Coefficient of Correlation
      Between Two Random Variables 15
   Summary 16
   Exercises 16

3. The Basic Theory 18
   The Repeated Measurement Experiment 18
   Measuring More Than One Person 28
   Further Consideration of
      True-Score and Error Variances 34
   Summary 35
   Exercises 36

4. Reliability 38
   Reliability Coefficient 38
   Uses of the Reliability Coefficient 39

| | Summary | 44 |
| | Exercises | 44 |

5.	Estimating the Reliability Coefficient	46
	Parallel Tests	46
	Reliability as a Correlation Coefficient	50
	Testing the Hypothesis of Parallel Tests	53
	Summary	62
	Exercises	65

6.	Experiments and Formulas for Estimating a Reliability Coefficient	66
	Factors to Consider in Conducting Reliability Experiments	66
	Estimating Reliability by Testing More Than Once	70
	Estimating Reliability by Testing Only Once	75
	Summary	94
	Exercises	96

7.	Factors Affecting the Reliability Coefficient	98
	Time Limits	98
	Test Length	99
	Item Characteristics	101
	Quality of the Scoring of Subjectively Scored Items	109
	Heterogeneity of the Population of Examinees	110
	Summary	110
	Exercises	112

8.	Estimating the Standard Error of Measurement	114
	Review and Comments	114
	Some Theory for the SEM	115
	A Practical but Flawed Approach	118
	A Better Approach	120
	Summary	121
	Exercises	124

9.	Special Topics Involving Reliability	126
	Reliability of Difference Scores	126
	Reliability Theory for Criterion-Referenced Measurements	138
	Summary	151
	Exercises	152

10. An Evaluation of
    Classical Reliability Theory   154

    Answers to Exercises   157
        Chapter 1   157
        Chapter 2   157
        Chapter 3   159
        Chapter 4   160
        Chapter 5   161
        Chapter 6   161
        Chapter 7   162
        Chapter 8   163
        Chapter 9   163

    References   165

    Author Index   168

    Subject Index   170

    About the Author   174

Series Editor's Introduction

Our conceptions of measurement reliability and available methods for estimating reliability statistics have advanced substantially in the past two decades. Classical test theory has been supplemented by mathematical models based on the random interchangeability of test items and tests. And models that differentiate among multiple sources of error, together with the computer programs needed to estimate model parameters, have become available to most measurement researchers. Nonetheless, classical models of examinees' performances on tests and other measures continue to have broad appeal and widespread application. The reasons are manifold. Many practical applications of social science measurement and educational testing involve quite small samples of examinees. The data needed to estimate the parameters of strong models of item-examinee interaction are not available in these situations, and the conditions of measurement preclude the kinds of differentiation among distinct sources of measurement error that generalizability approaches to assessing measurement consistency and stability require (see Shavelson & Webb, 1991).

In this volume, Ross E. Traub presents a finely crafted introduction to the theory and application of classical approaches to measurement reliability. Traub builds the case carefully and with consummate lucidity. He begins with a fundamental discussion of the concept and meaning of reliability—in everyday life and in social science measurement. He then takes a brief detour for the purpose of reviewing basic statistical concepts that are essential to a full understanding of the theoretical arguments advanced in the book. The following chapters provide a thorough grounding in theoretical foundations of classical test theory and reliability, and then Traub turns to practical approaches to the estimation of reliability and its associated statistics. Throughout the volume, close attention is paid to theoretical assumptions and to the consequences of their violation. All proofs, however, are constrained to sidebar sections that readers can set aside without loss of continuity, until they are ready to engage seriously in the mathematics of classical test theory. For those most interested in applications, Traub provides myriad worked examples that draw upon small, but realistic data sets. Readers are thus provided with step-by-step solutions of the most important practical problems that arise in estimating the reliability of social science measures.

Assessment of the reliability of difference scores, profiles, and criterion-referenced measurements round out the presentation and ensure that it is thoroughly up to date. Traub concludes the volume with a brief evaluation of classical approaches to measurement reliability, in contrast to alternative methods that have entered the measurement literature more recently.

Although this book examines a subject that has been explored many times, it is unique in its clarity, completeness, and craftsmanship. Many users of social science measurements who must understand basic indicators of measurement quality will find this book to be uniquely readable. It requires a minimum of mathematical preparation (in its most complex sections, the book requires no more than a course in basic algebra). In sum, *Reliability for the Social Sciences: Theory and Applications* is faithful to the goal of the **Measurement Methods for the Social Sciences** series, to make complex measurement concepts, topics, and methods accessible to readers who have limited mathematical backgrounds but a keen desire to understand and use methods that characterize the best of social science assessment.

RICHARD M. JAEGER
University of North Carolina at Greensboro

Preface

Reliability theory is a system of assumptions and theorems pertaining to variation in measurements. The theory was derived for scores on educational and psychological tests, but there is nothing in the tenets of the theory that limits its application to test scores. Reliability theory offers a way of thinking about, and a means of describing and evaluating the quality of, the numbers produced by the measuring procedures invented and employed by social scientists.

Several other scholars have published accounts of reliability theory. The bulk of Harold Gulliksen's (1950) book, *Theory of Mental Tests*, is addressed to reliability theory. Seven of the 24 chapters of *Statistical Theories of Mental Test Scores* by F. M. Lord and M. R. Novick (1968) are mostly about reliability theory. D. N. M. de Gruijter and L. J. Th. van der Kamp (1984) covered the topic in various parts of their text, *Statistical Models in Psychological and Educational Testing. Introduction to Classical & Modern Test Theory* by L. Crocker and J. Algina (1986), as its title implies, presents classical reliability theory, and more. The recent chapter by L. Feldt and R. Brennan (1989) on reliability in the third edition of *Educational Measurement* covers basic reliability theory (and much more).

Given the existence of the aforementioned publications, is there a need for yet another treatment of reliability theory? The answer is yes for at least two reasons. One reason is accessibility to an audience not well-schooled in mathematics and statistics. A second reason derives from the issue of scope of coverage. The treatments of reliability theory mentioned above differ among themselves in degree of mathematical and statistical sophistication assumed of the reader and also in scope of coverage. But all these publications, with the possible exception of Gulliksen's book, assume greater technical sophistication than the present work. And they all provide far greater breadth of coverage of test theory than the treatment offered here. The objective for the present work is to provide a concise and relatively nontechnical introduction to the concepts and applications of basic reliability theory.

Why should social science students need or want such a treatment of reliability theory as this? An answer to this question follows straightforwardly for social science students who will be using or referring to quantitative data in their research. It is important for these individuals to understand that error is associated with the measurements or observations that produce quantitative data, and to know at least some of the implications this understanding entails.

In preparing this book, I benefited from, and here gratefully acknowledge, the assistance of several individuals: Glenn Rowley helped frame the original outline for the volume and influenced the final product greatly through our collaborations on several previous publications. Penny McCormick read three drafts of the manuscript from the perspective of someone in the audience for whom the book is intended; she identified numerous obscurities in the development and explication of concepts, and challenged my thinking about ideas that are not easy for the tyro social scientist either to grasp or to accept. Comments and criticisms from James Algina, Michal Beller, Michael Maraun, an unknown reviewer, and Series Editor Richard Jaeger, helped improve the organization, the writing, and the correctness of the material. None of these people, however, should be held responsible for deficiencies in the final product.

1

Introduction

Reliability is used in everyday speech to describe persons or things. A reliable person can be counted on, hence a reliable employee turns up for work on time and performs assigned duties to the best of her or his abilities. A reliable machine performs as expected each time it is used, so we call an automobile reliable if the motor starts every time the key is turned in the ignition and it rarely, if ever, breaks down. Reliability is also used to describe a particular quality of the numbers obtained by measuring the characteristics of persons or things. In this usage, just as in everyday parlance, reliability connotes a kind of consistency, here of the measurements being described.

The purpose of this book is to develop the concept of reliability with reference to educational and psychological measurements—the scores that result when a test or questionnaire is administered to one person or more. The concept of reliability has been developed in a line of work that can be traced back at least to the Scottish psychologist, Charles Spearman (1904, 1907). Added to by various contributors over the years, a formal and systematic statement of reliability theory was presented by the American educational statistician Melvin Novick (1966; Lord & Novick, 1968, chaps. 1 & 2).

A Word About Measurement

Before delving into reliability theory, we pause to consider the concept of measurement, for, as has been noted, reliability theory pertains to the numbers we call measurements. According to *Merriam-Webster's Collegiate Dictionary* (10th ed., 1993), *measurement* connotes both "the act or process of measuring" and "a figure, extent, or

1

amount obtained by measuring." In this book, attention is focused on the numbers resulting from an act or process of measuring, with a view to assessing the quality of the measurements and, if necessary and practicable, improving the process.

And how are we to describe the act or process of measuring? A useful starting point is the dictum of S. S. Stevens (1948). He declared measurement to be the process of assigning numbers to objects or persons according to rules. The modifications we would make to Stevens's definition were suggested by Jones (1971), who noted (1) that measurements are of *characteristics* of objects or persons, not of objects or persons per se, and (2) that measurements convey information about the *amount* of the characteristic possessed by an object or person. Jones's first qualification rules out the use of numbers to indicate only that two or more persons are different, as in the use of numbers to identify the players on a baseball team. His second qualification excludes the use of numbers to designate eye color (e.g., 1 blue, 2 brown, 3 green, etc.), for the differences between numbers used in this way tell us nothing about how persons differ quantitatively in amount of eye color. Jones's second qualification also rules out the use of numbers to indicate only rank order in the amount of a characteristic possessed by two or more persons, as in the use of rank-in-class to indicate academic merit, for again a difference in rank tells us nothing about the size of the difference in amount of the characteristic being measured. Stevens accepted the latter two uses of numbers as primitive forms of measurement, which he called, respectively, measurement on a nominal scale and measurement on an ordinal scale. Jones's requirements for measuring are satisfied by what Stevens called measurement on interval scales and measurement on ratio scales—scales of the former type have an arbitrarily defined zero point and are best exemplified by thermometers for measuring temperature, whereas scales of the latter type have a naturally defined zero point and are best exemplified by the scales used for measuring distance.

In social science, much of measurement consists of assigning numbers by referring to the responses persons give to a test or questionnaire. The assigned number may be nothing more than a count of the correct responses made by the examinee to the items in a multiple-choice test or the number of points a reader assigns to an essay written by the examinee. This count or number of points is thought to reflect in some sense the *amount* of knowledge or ability possessed by the examinee. Reliability theory is not inherently limited to measurements of this sort;

it is applicable to the numbers assigned by any rule-driven process to a characteristic of persons or things, provided only that the scale involved is either of the interval or ratio variety in Stevens's typology.

The measurements used in social science research and in the applications made of social science should be of the highest quality. The theory presented in this book provides the foundation for procedures by which the reliability of sets of measurements can be assessed. If the measurements in a set are found to be of low reliability, then steps should be taken to improve the measuring process. Readers are forewarned, however, that an assessment of the reliability of a set of measurements is unlikely to pinpoint the improvements needed. Still, several basic principles based on classical reliability theory suggest general strategies for improving a measuring procedure. These are considered later.

The reason why classical reliability theory cannot be used to identify the flaws in a measuring process lies in the fact that educational and psychological measures usually involve persons responding to stimuli of some kind (e.g., students answer questions testing knowledge of physics). Developing an educational or psychological measure requires more than knowing how to assess the technical adequacy of the measurements produced. An understanding is also required of how persons respond to test questions. The improvement of measuring procedures, when improvements are called for, invariably requires the efforts of psychologists who understand the nature of the human response process elicited by a particular measuring procedure, as well as contributions from specialists in the subject matter being tested and persons schooled in measurement theory.

Alternatives to classical reliability theory exist. Previously published volumes in this series have presented two alternatives: Generalizability theory (Shavelson & Webb, 1991) and item response theory (Hambleton, Swaminathan, & Rogers, 1991). Aspects of these alternatives are noted from time to time in this volume, to help distinguish classical theory from generalizability theory and item response theory and also to prepare interested readers for the study of these alternatives.

Overview

The remainder of the book is divided into nine chapters. The statistical concepts of a random variable and the expected value of a random variable underlie the presentation offered here. These fundamental concepts are developed in Chapter 2. The third chapter is an outline of the basic tenets of classical reliability theory. Chapter 4 gives the technical definition of reliability as a coefficient, and illustrates possible uses of the coefficient. The notion of parallel tests is considered in Chapter 5; this notion is important because it links theory to reality, making possible the estimation of a reliability coefficient for a set of measurements. Consideration is also given in Chapter 5 to the situation that pertains when parallel tests, or approximately parallel tests, are not available. Ways of estimating the reliability of sets of measurement are reviewed in Chapter 6. The seventh chapter consists of a discussion of factors that can affect the reliability coefficient. In the eighth chapter consideration is given to the matter of estimating the standard error of measurement, a statistic that complements the reliability coefficient. The final two chapters are focused, respectively, on several special topics and on an evaluation of classical reliability theory. Bibliographic references are provided at the end of the book.

Two additional points about the organization of the book: (1) Sidebars have been included at irregular intervals. Some sidebars contain discussions intended to further your understanding of particular concepts. Other sidebars provide algebraic proofs of assertions made in the text. The material in the sidebars can be ignored on first reading, but the sidebars should be studied closely at some point by readers who wish to acquire more than a superficial understanding of classical reliability theory. (2) Most chapters conclude with exercises. These are intended both to assist the reader assess his or her understanding of the material presented in the chapter and to promote the development of a deeper understanding of this material. Answers to the exercises are provided at the end of the book.

Exercise

1.1. Describe two situations, different from those mentioned in the text, in which the notion of reliability as consistency can be seen to apply.

2

A Brief Statistical Interlude

In modern treatments of reliability theory, measurements are viewed as observations of a *random variable*. The purpose of this chapter is to build conceptions of the terms *random variable, expected value* of a random variable, *variance* of a random variable, and *covariance* of two random variables. Readers familiar with these terms can proceed directly to Chapter 3. Others should read this chapter before going on.

Variable

In nontechnical terms, a *variable* is a characteristic of the objects of measurement, a characteristic that can assume any one of a specified set of outcomes. The characteristics or variables of interest in reliability theory are quantitative in nature, hence the sets of outcomes for these variables are real numbers (points on the number line). We refer to these numbers as measurements. For example, height possesses the qualities of a quantitative variable; it is a characteristic of people for which measurements are expressed as real numbers. The set of possible measurements for the height of an adult includes the numbers ranging from somewhat less than 60 inches to somewhat more than 84 inches. Other examples of quantitative variables are weight and income. The numerical outcomes for any of these characteristics can be different for the individuals who are the objects of measurement. Indeed, the numerical outcomes can even differ from one measurement to another of the same person. This variation in measurements, whether from one person to another or from one measurement to another of the same person, is aptly captured by the term *variable*.

As has been noted, the variables listed in the previous paragraph are *quantitative* in nature and are to be distinguished from variables that are *categorical* in nature. Gender, blood type, country of birth, and eye color (previously considered in Chapter 1) are examples of categorical variables. The possible outcomes for variables such as these also can be represented by numbers, so if gender is the variable of interest, females might be assigned the number 2 and males the number 1. But these numbers are assigned arbitrarily and serve merely to denote membership, either in the class of females or that of males. In particular, these numbers do not denote relative amount of gender, so they are not quantitative measurements in the sense considered in Chapter 1.

Debate has raged in the literature of quantitative social science as to whether test scores, consisting, for example, of the number of test questions answered correctly, qualify as quantitative variables. From one perspective, test scores define nothing more than the pigeonholes of a categorical variable and, as such, merely provide measurements on a nominal scale. From another perspective, test scores are viewed as defining a rank order on the characteristic being measured, and so embody the characteristics of an ordinal scale. From yet another perspective, however, test scores are viewed as quantitative variables, with any difference in the test scores of two persons—two observations of the variable—reflecting the difference in *amounts* of the characteristic possessed by these measured persons. As noted in Chapter 1, the focus of attention in the present discussion of reliability theory is on variables presumed to be quantitative in nature, not on those presumed to be categorical.

Random Variable

A variable is described as *random* if the numerical values observed of the variable can be said to result from the operation of a chance process, that is, a process not under the control of the person observing the variable. Consider, for example, a study of intelligence. This variable is observed by administering a test to a person. An intelligence test score can be viewed as the realization of a two-part random process: First, a person must be chosen for testing. A selection process that clearly involves the operation of a chance process is one in which a lottery is used to choose examinees. Most research in the social sciences does not involve the study of persons chosen by lottery, but if the researcher does not set out to test particular individuals, then the choice of a person for testing can be, and usually is, viewed as a chance event.

The second sense in which an intelligence test score is a random event is this: The score a person will obtain is unknown before the test is administered. It is true, of course, that some persons, if tested, will achieve high scores and others will achieve low scores. Regardless of this fact, however, any person who is tested might obtain any one of a set of different scores on the intelligence test. It is possible to imagine that, were circumstances different from those prevailing at the time the test was administered, a different score might have been obtained. Suppose, for example, the test were administered on a different day or at a different time of day, when the examinee's motivation and also his or her capacity to respond might be greater or smaller; clearly, a different test score might well result. Which degree of motivation and capacity to respond are involved at the time the test is administered is, according to this analysis, a matter of chance.

Some notational conventions are followed in writing about random variables. The variables themselves are often symbolized by italicized capital letters of the ordinary alphabet. In this book, we use such symbols as "X" and "E" to refer to random variables. Particular observations of the random variable are symbolized as lower case letters. For example, "x" and "e" stand, respectively, for observations of the random variables X and E. The expression "$X = x$" denotes the fact that an observation has been taken of the random variable X, with outcome or measurement x being realized. Although the particular value of x is not defined in the foregoing expression, it could be any one of the set of possible values that a random variable X can take. For example, if the set of possible values for X were $\{10, 11, 12, 13, 14, 15\}$, then x could be any one, but only one, of the numbers $10, 11, \ldots, 15$.

Expected Value of a Random Variable

This concept is analogous to the arithmetic mean of a set of measurements. But the expected value differs from the arithmetic mean in that the latter is calculated for a set of numbers using a familiar rule—sum all the numbers, then divide this total by the number of numbers summed— whereas the former is derived using the probability distribution for the random variable. This explanation is no help, of course, without knowing both what a probability distribution is and the kind of derivation needed.

The idea of a probability distribution is illustrated in Figure 2.1. The histogram depicted in this figure was derived initially from 200 numbers, assumed to be the outcomes of 200 repetitions of the process of measuring the length of a table's top. These 200 numbers have an arithmetic mean of 48 inches. Suppose, however, we forget how the histogram was obtained, and scale the figure so that the area covered by all the bars of the histogram is exactly one square unit. (We can do this by dividing the observed frequency of each measurement by 200; the resulting numbers are relative frequencies.) Then the area of the bar for each possible measurement for the table's top is a fraction of one, and as such possesses a property of the numbers we refer to as probabilities; any such number must be greater than or equal to zero and less than or equal to one (refer to the scale along the right-hand side of Figure 2.1). Moreover, the set of areas corresponding to all the different measurements possible for the table's top possesses another property of probabilities; they total 1. From the probability perspective, then, we can view Figure 2.1 as the *probability distribution* of the random variable that is observed whenever the table top is measured. In other words, Figure 2.1 enables us to evaluate the probability that the next measurement we make of the table will turn out to be one or another of the values in the set of all possible measurements, which set includes the numbers 47.95, 47.96, . . . , 48.05. For example, the probability that the next observation is 48.03 inches is .05, or 1 chance in 20.

Now let X represent the random variable that is observed whenever the top of the table is measured and let P_x represent the probability associated with each measurement $X = x$ that might be observed. We can calculate the *expected value of the random variable X* by employing the operations indicated in Table 2.1. The expected value of X is by definition $\sum(P_x x)$, where $\sum$ here means "sum the products of P_x and x over all possible values of $X = x$."

To see that the expected value of a random variable is analogous to the sample mean, note that the column of probabilities, P_x, in Table 2.1 can be viewed as the *relative frequencies* of the corresponding measurements $X = x$. Thus each product $(P_x x)$ is analogous to the sum of all the measurements that are exactly $X = x$ (e.g., $X = 48.01$ is associated with the sum 8.40175). The overall sum, namely $\sum(P_x x)$, is therefore analogous to the numerator of the expression for calculating the mean of a set of numbers. The sum of the relative frequencies $\sum P_x$ is 1, as it must be if the set of numbers {48.05, 48.04, . . . , 47.95} includes all the different numbers it is possible to realize in measuring the length of the table's top. To pursue the analogy to the sample mean, the denominator of the expression for the expected value of X is also $\sum P_x$, that is, 1. Thus the expected value $\varepsilon(X)$ or analogue of the mean is

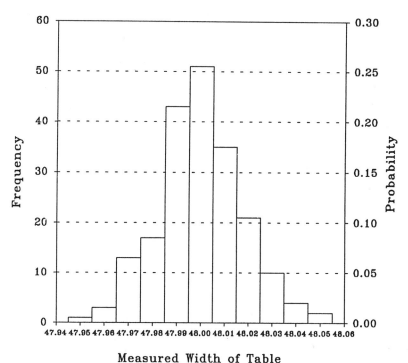

Figure 2.1. The Frequency Histogram of 200 Measurements of a Table Top. If the relative frequency of each measurement is calculated (by dividing the observed frequency of the measurement by 200) and if we assume this relative frequency is the probability that this particular measurement will be obtained when the table is next measured, then we can interpret the histogram as the probability distribution of the random variable that is observed when the table is measured (see the scale on the right-hand margin of the figure).

$$\varepsilon(X) = \frac{\sum_x (P_x x)}{\sum_x (P_x)} = \sum_x (P_x x) .$$

For the random variable of Figure 2.1, the expected value is 48.00 inches.

TABLE 2.1 Calculation of the Expected Value of the Random Variable With the Probability Distribution Given in Figure 2.1

x	P_x	$P_x x$
48.05	0.010	0.48050
48.04	0.020	0.96080
48.03	0.050	2.40150
48.02	0.105	5.04210
48.01	0.175	8.40175
48.00	0.255	12.24000
47.99	0.215	10.31785
47.98	0.085	4.07830
47.97	0.065	3.11805
47.96	0.015	0.71940
47.95	0.005	0.23975
	$\sum P_x$	$\sum (P_x x)$
	$= 1.00$	$= \varepsilon(X)$
		$= 48.00$

It is common practice to use the lower case Greek letter μ (mu), sometimes with a subscript to designate the random variable, to symbolize the expected value of a random variable, thus for the random variable X:

$$\mu_X = \varepsilon(X) = \sum_x (P_x x) . \qquad (2.1)$$

Table 2.1 illustrates the calculation of the expected value of a *discrete random variable*. The process of measuring the length of a table top might seem to involve a continuous random variable, because any possible point on the number line over the full range of the random variable might be observed. In practice, however, the measurements taken of the length of a table top are discrete, due to the fact that they are recorded to the nearest unit determined by (1) the distance between the marks on the ruler being used and (2) the visual acuity of the person taking the measurements. For Figure 2.1, the distance between marks on the ruler was, presumably, 0.01 inch, and the measurer's visual acuity was sufficient to judge the table's length on each measurement to the nearest 0.01 of an inch.

If a variable is truly continuous, we still can determine its expected value, provided we know its probability distribution, referred to in this case by the special name, *probability density*. We use an adjusted version of the procedure used in obtaining the expected value of a discrete variable (see, e.g., Keeping, 1962).

The expected value of a random variable is but one example of what statisticians call the *moments of a random variable*. In this case, the moments are referred to the origin or zero point on the scale used in taking the measurements. Expected values referred to the origin for discrete random variables have the general form $\sum(P_x x^r)$, where r, which can be any positive integer, defines the order of the moment under consideration. When r is set to 1, we have the first moment referred to the origin, namely the expected value of the random variable. Other moments with reference to the origin can be defined by setting r to some other positive integer, but in this work we are only interested in the first moment referred to the origin.

The Variance of a Random Variable

There is another class of moments that is of interest to statisticians, namely moments referred to the expected value of the random variable. Moments of this kind have the form

$$\varepsilon[X - \varepsilon(X)]^r \equiv \varepsilon[X - \mu_X]^r.$$

For discrete random variables, this expression becomes

$$\varepsilon[X - \varepsilon(X)]^r = \sum\{P_x[x - \varepsilon(X)]^r\}$$

$$= \sum\{P_x[x - \sum(P_x x)]^r\}$$

$$= \sum\{P_x[x - \mu_X]^r\}, \tag{2.2}$$

where r is again any positive integer, $\mu_X = \varepsilon(X) = \sum(P_x x)$, and the summation $\sum$ is over all possible values of $X = x$. Because $\varepsilon(X) = \mu_X$ is called the mean of the random variable, moments of the form $\varepsilon[X - \varepsilon(X)]^r$ are commonly known as moments referred to the mean. Of most interest to us is the second moment referred to the mean, that is

TABLE 2.2 Calculation of the Variance and Standard Deviation of the Random
Variable With the Probability Distribution Given in Figure 2.1

x	P_x	$x - \mu$	$(x - \mu)^2$	$P_x(x - \mu)^2$
48.05	0.010	0.05	0.0025	0.0000250
48.04	0.020	0.04	0.0016	0.0000320
48.03	0.050	0.03	0.0009	0.0000450
48.02	0.105	0.02	0.0004	0.0000420
48.01	0.175	0.01	0.0001	0.0000175
48.00	0.255	0.00	0.0000	0.0000000
47.99	0.215	−0.01	0.0001	0.0000215
47.98	0.085	−0.02	0.0004	0.0000340
47.97	0.065	−0.03	0.0009	0.0000585
47.96	0.015	−0.04	0.0016	0.0000240
47.95	0.005	−0.05	0.0025	0.0000125

$$\sum P_x(x - \mu)^2 = \sigma_X^2 = 0.000312$$
$$\sigma_X = 0.018$$

$$\varepsilon[X - \varepsilon(X)]^2 = \sum \{ P_x[x - \mu_X]^2 \}. \tag{2.3}$$

This is called the variance of the random variable X and is symbolized
σ_X^2. (The symbol σ is the lower case Greek letter sigma.) The calculation
of the variance of the random variable with the probability distribution
given in Figure 2.1 is illustrated in Table 2.2. Often we also are
interested in the standard deviation of a random variable, which is
readily obtained by taking the square root of the variance.

It is shown in Sidebar 2.1 that an alternative expression for the
variance, one equivalent to Equation 2.3, is as follows:

$$\sigma_X^2 = \varepsilon(X^2) - (\mu_X)^2 = \sum (P_x x^2) - [\sum (P_x x)]^2. \tag{2.4}$$

The Covariance of Two Random Variables

Another concept that can be defined in expected-value terms is the
covariance of two random variables. Suppose each time an object is
examined we measure two of its characteristics. This is what would occur,
for example, if both the length of a table and its height were measured each

---

Sidebar 2.1

A PROOF OF THE EQUALITY OF TWO EXPRESSIONS FOR THE VARIANCE OF A RANDOM VARIABLE

Our requirement is to show the equivalence of Equations 2.3 and 2.4. By definition from Equation 2.3,

$$\sigma_X^2 = \varepsilon(X - \mu_X)^2. \tag{2.1.1}$$

If we square the expression in parentheses on the right-hand side of Equation 2.1.1, we obtain the following result:

$$\sigma_X^2 = \varepsilon[X^2 - 2X\mu_X + \mu_X^2]. \tag{2.1.2}$$

Now the expectation operator has the property that it can be distributed over the terms in square brackets on the right-hand side of Equation 2.1.2, resulting in the following expression:

$$\sigma_X^2 = \varepsilon(X^2) - \varepsilon(2X\mu_X) + \varepsilon(\mu_X^2). \tag{2.1.3}$$

Now the expectation of a constant is the constant itself. Inasmuch as the numeral 2 and the mean μ_X are constants, we can rewrite Equation 2.1.3 as follows:

$$\sigma_X^2 = \varepsilon(X^2) - (2\mu_X)\varepsilon(X) + \mu_X^2$$

$$= \varepsilon(X^2) - (2\mu_X)\mu_X + \mu_X^2$$

$$= \varepsilon(X^2) - 2\mu_X^2 + \mu_X^2$$

$$= \varepsilon(X^2) - \mu_X^2. \tag{2.1.4}$$

This is the first part of Equation 2.4.
For a discrete random variable, $\varepsilon(X^2) = \sum(P_x x^2)$ by definition. Also $\mu_X^2 = [\sum(P_x x)]^2$. When these results are substituted in Equation 2.1.4, we obtain the second part of Equation 2.4.

---

time measurements were taken of the table. Let Y represent the random variable observed in measuring the height of the table, and let P_y denote the probability that the outcome of the process of measuring the table's height is the measurement $Y = y$. Clearly, Y has an expected value, which we denote as $\varepsilon(Y) = \sum(P_y y) = \mu_Y$, and a variance, which we denote as $\sigma_Y^2 = \varepsilon[Y - \varepsilon(Y)]^2 = \varepsilon[Y - \mu_Y]^2 = \sum\{P_y[y - \mu_Y]^2\}$.

The covariance is an index of the degree to which there exists an association between the X and Y random variables. For example, if we were to measure both the length and height of a table many times, and were to observe (1) that every time a relatively large length measurement was obtained, a relatively large height measurement was obtained, (2) that every time a middling length measurement was recorded, a middling height measurement was recorded, and (3) that every time a relatively small length measurement was observed, a relatively small height measurement was observed, then we would have discovered a positive association between the measurements of length and height. Moreover, the covariance of height and weight measurements in this example would be positive. It is possible to imagine situations with negative associations or covariances between two variables and others with no association or covariation whatsoever.

When studying covariation, we are interested in all possible joint occurrences of the values of two random variables. Returning again to the example involving the length and height of a table, each different combination that is possible for values $X = x$ of the length random variable and values $Y = y$ of the height random variable is associated with a probability of their joint occurrence, say P_{xy}. The covariance of length measurements X and height measurements Y is then defined to be

$$\sigma_{XY} = \varepsilon[(X - \mu_X)(Y - \mu_Y)] = \sum[P_{xy}(x - \mu_X)(y - \mu_Y)], \qquad (2.5)$$

where the expectation operator ε and the summation operator $\sum$ both involve all possible combinations of pairs of values $X = x$ and $Y = y$. Table 2.3 illustrates the calculation of σ_{XY} for hypothetical data in which there are only three possible length measurements and only three possible height measurements, hence only nine possible combinations of the values of length and height. Note that in this example the covariance is zero between measurements of the length and height of a table. Thus we can conclude there is no association between the measurements of the length and the measurements of the height of the table.

Using an argument analogous to that used in Sidebar 2.1, it can be shown that the covariance between two variables can also be expressed as follows:

$$\sigma_{XY} = \sum[P_{xy}(xy)] - \mu_X\mu_Y, \qquad (2.6)$$

TABLE 2.3 Calculation of the Covariance of Two Random Variables

x,y	P_{xy}	$(x - \mu_X)(y - \mu_Y)$	$P_{xy}(x - \mu_X)(y - \mu_Y)$
48.01, 36.01	0.05	(0.01)(0.01)	0.000005
48.01, 36.00	0.15	(0.01)(0.00)	0.000000
48.01, 35.99	0.05	(0.01)(−0.01)	−0.000005
48.00, 36.01	0.10	(0.00)(0.01)	0.000000
48.00, 36.00	0.30	(0.00)(0.00)	0.000000
48.00, 35.99	0.10	(0.00)(−0.01)	0.000000
47.99, 36.01	0.05	(−0.01)(0.01)	−0.000005
47.99, 36.00	0.10	(−0.01)(0.00)	0.000000
47.99, 35.99	0.05	(−0.01)(−0.01)	0.000005
	$\sum P_{xy} = 1.00$		

$$\sigma_{XY} = \varepsilon[(X - \mu_X)(Y - \mu_Y)]$$
$$= \sum[P_{xy}(x - \mu_X)(y - \mu_Y)]$$
$$= 0.000000$$

where $\sum[P_{xy}(xy)]$ is the sum over all possible combinations of values $X = x$ and $Y = y$, and $[P_{xy}(xy)]$ is the product of P_{xy}, x, and y.

The Coefficient of Correlation Between Two Random Variables

A standardized index of the degree of association between two random variables is the Pearson product-moment coefficient of correlation. This entity is defined as the covariance of the variables divided by the product of the standard deviations of the variables. In symbolic form,

$$\rho_{XY} = \frac{\sigma_{XY}}{\sigma_X \sigma_Y}, \tag{2.7}$$

where ρ_{XY} is the symbol used to denote the coefficient of correlation between random variables X and Y, and the other symbols are defined as before. For example, if $\sigma_{XY} = 55$, $\sigma_X = 10$, and $\sigma_Y = 10$, then $\rho_{XY} = 0.55$. The coefficient ρ_{XY} is described as standardized because it must be some number in the range −1 to 1, inclusive. The extreme values represent relationships between X and Y that are perfect in the sense that when observations of X are plotted against corresponding observations of Y, the plotted points all lie on a straight line. Thus a coefficient of 1 denotes a perfect increasing straight-line relationship between X and Y, whereas a coefficient of −1 denotes a perfect decreasing straight-line relationship between the two variables. Values of ρ_{XY} larger than -1 but smaller than 1 are typical of social science variables, and denote relationships for which the plotted points scatter about a straight line that defines how one variable changes relative to changes in the other. A coefficient of 0 defines another extreme, that is, two variables for which the plot of observations of X against corresponding observations of Y defines no discernable increasing or decreasing straight-line relationship. (For a more detailed discussion of the correlation coefficient see any standard statistics textbook, such as that by Marascuilo & Serlin, 1988.)

Summary

A random variable is any characteristic of the members of a well-defined population, with the proviso that the next member of the population to be studied—the next observation of the random variable—is determined by chance. If the random variable is quantitative but discrete (as opposed to continuous), and if we know the probabilities of occurrence for every possible measurement (number) that the random variable can assume, then the expected value of the random variable and its variance can be calculated by applying Equations 2.1 and 2.3. These considerations make it possible to deal with test scores and other measurements in social science as random variables. Moreover, when two random variables are involved, it is possible, given knowledge of the probabilities associated with the joint occurrence of each possible pair of measurements (outcomes) of the two random variables, to calculate the covariance of the variables using Equations 2.5 or 2.6 and the coefficient of correlation of the two random variables using Equation 2.7.

Exercises

2.1. A coin toss results in an observation of a random variable, one with only two possible outcomes, head and tail. If the occurrence of a head is scored 1 and the occurrence of a tail is scored 2, what is the expected value of this random variable? (Assume that the coin is fair in the sense that the outcomes, head and tail, are equally likely.)

2.2. What is the variance of the random variable described in Exercise 2.1?

2.3. The probability distribution for observations of the random variable IQ (with measurements rounded to the nearest IQ score that is divisible by 10) is given in the following table:

IQ	P_x
70	0.0475
80	0.1112
90	0.2120
100	0.2586
110	0.2120
120	0.1112
130	0.0475

Calculate the expected value and the variance of the IQ random variable with the foregoing probability distribution.

2.4. Given the following table of information about the joint occurrence of two random variables in a population of persons, compute the covariance of the two variables and the coefficient of correlation between them.

x	y	P_{xy}
4	1	0.00
4	2	0.00
4	3	0.05
4	4	0.10
3	1	0.00
3	2	0.10
3	3	0.20
3	4	0.05
2	1	0.05
2	2	0.20
2	3	0.10
2	4	0.00
1	1	0.10
1	2	0.05
1	3	0.00
1	4	0.00

(Hint: You need to compute the expected values and the variances of the variables X and Y, as well as their covariance. To do this, you need to obtain probability distributions for random variables X and Y individually. These are referred to as the marginal distributions. They can be obtained from the information provided about the joint probability distribution of X and Y by putting the given values of P_{xy} in a two-way table and summing rows and columns of the table to obtain the different values of P_x and P_y that are required.)

3

The Basic Theory

Reliability theory derives from the consideration of several random variables: one for observed measurements, also called observed scores; another for true scores; and yet another for errors of measurement or error scores. So that these concepts can be easily understood, they are developed first in the context of a practical example of measurement, that of determining the length of a table top. Subsequently, the ideas are related to measurements derived from educational and psychological tests and questionnaires, and other procedures used in social science research of the quantitative kind.

The Repeated Measurement Experiment

We begin by conducting a simple thought experiment. Imagine measuring the length of a table top over and over again. If the markings on the ruler used to make the measurements are sufficiently close together so that the measurements are obtained to, say, the nearest one-hundredth of an inch, then the repeated measurements will include several different numbers. Two hundred such repetitions might produce the numbers used to form the histogram displayed earlier in Figure 2.1. Two features of Figure 2.1 are worthy of notice: (1) The measurements vary quite considerably, from a low of 47.95 inches to a high of 48.05 inches, and (2) measurements in close proximity to 48.00 inches occur far more frequently than do measurements at either extreme of the histogram.

At this point we are faced with a problem: What do we say the length of the table top is? Had we made only one measurement, we would declare the length of the table top to be equal to the single number obtained. But with many different measurements and no reason to think any one of them better than another, we might decide to compute their arithmetic mean, and report it as the best or most typical or (in some sense) *true* length of the table. Then the difference between any one of the measurements and the arithmetic mean might be described as a departure or a deviation from the best or most typical or true length; this difference might be described as the *error* made in measuring the table on that occasion.

The ideas in the foregoing paragraph offer a useful way of describing measurements, but they are not theoretically precise. The arithmetic mean of 200 measurements is really nothing more than a complicated kind of observed score, one derived from elementary observed scores. Moreover, this mean will itself almost certainly differ from the true length of the table, which we can never know, by an amount that also can never be known. This theoretical problem can be circumvented by redefining *true score* as the *expected value* of the *random variable* that is observed whenever the length of the table top is measured. An error score now can be defined as the difference between an observed measurement and the true score. We will see that this conception of true score and error score makes possible a precise definition of reliability. With the addition of several assumptions, it is also possible to devise ways of estimating the reliability of sets of measurements.

The foregoing developments can be summarized for the measurement of a characteristic of a *person* as follows: Let X_p be the random variable that is observed whenever characteristic X of person p is measured. Then, an observation of the random variable is thought to be composed of two parts: (1) the expected value of the random variable, which is referred to as the *true score*; and (2) the difference between the observed score and the true score, which is called the *error score* or the *error of measurement*. This partition of the observed score, say $X_p = x_p$ for person p, into a true score, say τ_p, and an error score, say $E_p = e_p$, can be stated as follows:

$$x_p = \tau_p + e_p \, . \tag{3.1}$$

Equation 3.1 is the *fundamental equation* of classical reliability theory. In mathematical terms, Equation 3.1 is a tautology, which is to say the sum of the two quantities on the right-hand side of the equation equals the single quantity on the left-hand side *by definition*. Consequently, the fundamental equation of classical reliability theory can never be proven false as a way of representing or modeling observed scores. Whether or not Equation 3.1 is accepted as valid depends on whether or not it seems reasonable to think of test scores and other measurements as consisting of the linear combination[1] of true-score and error-score components.

Note that we have symbolized the true score as τ_p, where, as before, p denotes the person being measured. The convention followed in this book is to use symbols of the Greek alphabet to refer to parameters (such as moments) of random variables. Inasmuch as the true score τ_p is the expected value of the person-specific random variable X_p, τ_p is a parameter of X_p and is appropriately designated by a letter (tau) of the Greek alphabet. The corresponding quantity for a sample of observations on a random variable is designated by a letter of the regular alphabet. Thus $\overline{X}_p$ is the mean of a sample of observations on the random variable X_p. (Subscripts, such as the p in τ_p, usually appear either as letters of the regular alphabet or as Arabic numerals; in isolated instances, for reasons that will be clear in context, letters of the Greek alphabet are sometimes also used as subscripts.)

We pause here to consider the notions of true score and error in greater detail.

True Score (Expected Value of the Person-Specific Random Variable X_p)

This entity, denoted τ_p, has been defined as the expected value of the random variable X_p that is observed whenever person p is measured by a test. Inasmuch as X_p is the observed-score random variable for person p, it is referred to hereafter as a *person-specific random variable,* to distinguish it from the random variables defined later for populations of examinees. One thing to note about τ_p is that it is unlikely to be a whole number, such as 63 on a vocabulary test of 75 questions, where each question is scored 0 for incorrect, 1 for correct. Instead, τ_p is likely to be some number such as 63.297. It should be obvious that an *observed* score of 63 questions correct on the aforementioned vocabulary test would be possible, but that an *observed* score of 63.297 questions correct would be impossible.

The true score being considered here is not an ideal score or *Platonic true score* such as that which might be thought useful for describing the extent of a student's knowledge of vocabulary. Consider, for example, the following vocabulary question: "What is a *trampoline?*" It is intuitively compelling to suppose that a student either knows the answer to this question or does not know it. In accord with this supposition is the view that the student's Platonic true score for the question is also discrete, being either 0 if the answer is unknown or 1 if known. But this view is deterministic and does not readily accommodate itself to the notion of error—error in the sense that the test scores for a student's answer to a vocabulary question very often will fluctuate, being 1 on one occasion, 0 on another. Score fluctuations can occur, for example, because states of knowledge fluctuate, such that a student knows the answer to a question on one occasion, but not on another. The notion of Platonic true score is discussed further in Sidebar 3.1.

As defined in classical reliability theory, a student's true score is the expected value of the person-specific random variable that is observed whenever the student is administered a test containing questions such as "What is a *trampoline*?" If the student's answer to this question were correct every time she encountered it in a test and if correct answers were always scored 1, then her expected-value true score for the question would also be 1. If, however, for whatever reason—momentary lapse of memory, confusion caused by fatigue—the student's answer could be incorrect on even one of the occasions when the question might be asked, then her expected-value true score for the question would be a number between 0 and 1 (because there is a nonzero probability of getting the answer wrong and scoring 0).

The foregoing example illustrates why the expected-value true score of a student for a single test item, which is scored 0 for incorrect and 1 for correct, will in general be a number between 0 and 1, inclusive. Continuing the argument of the foregoing example, a student's expected-value true score for a test containing several vocabulary questions can be expected to be any point on the segment of the real number line from 0 to n, where n is the number of items on the test.

The foregoing conception of repeated measurements applies to situations in which the measurements that can possibly be observed on a given repetition vary over a range of values on the number line. An administration of a 50-item achievement test, with the test score being the sum of "0" and "1" item scores (for incorrect and correct answers, respectively), could in principle yield a score equal to any whole number in the range from 0 to 50 inclusive. If we gave the identical test repeatedly to a single person, however, we would expect the measurements for that particular person to range more narrowly, over some small portion of the 0 to 50 score scale. Figure 3.1 illustrates possible probability

Sidebar 3.1

AN EXTENDED DISCUSSION OF PLATONIC TRUE SCORE

The *Platonic true score* is not an average or expected value. Instead, it is the measurement that an object really should be assigned on the characteristic being measured. The association intended from the name, Platonic true score, is the world of ideal forms discussed by the Greek philosopher Plato.

An example, considered at some length by Lord and Novick (1968), arises from the process used to determine the sex of newly hatched chicks. If a chick is allowed to develop into an adult chicken, its sex will be obvious, hen or rooster, female or male. But the sex of a newly hatched chick is not obvious. To fill an order for, say, 100 female chicks, a hatchery will have newly hatched chicks examined by experienced judges. Those chicks judged to be females will be used to fill the order.

The judgments of a chick's sex are fallible, so mistakes are made. As chicks mature, the mistakes become obvious—the roosters that develop from chicks thought at the time of hatching to be females.

To put all this in the context of a Platonic conception of true score versus the expected-value conception of true score inherent in classical reliability theory, consider the possibility that the sex of a newly hatched chick is judged either by a great many different judges or by the same judge a great many times. The resulting judgments will be of a random variable, namely the judged sex of the chick. The true score for the chick in the sense of classical reliability theory is the expected value of this random variable, estimated in practice as the average of all the judgments made of the sex of a particular chick. If the judgment "female" were scored 2 and the judgment "male" were scored 1, then the estimated true score of a chick would be a number in the range from 1 to 2, inclusive. The estimated true score would be exactly 1 or exactly 2 only if the judgments of the chick's sex were all the same (either all 1s or all 2s). On the other hand, the Platonic true score for the chick is its actual sex, which is not determined by anyone's judgments. The Platonic true score is not an expected value of a random variable, but is the sex the chick really possesses.

In the context of assessing educational achievement, if the state of a person's knowledge is presumed to be constant and immutable, even for a very short time, then it is reasonable to think of the true score for the person on a test in Platonic terms. The person either will know or will not know the answer to every question, and the true score is exactly equal to the number of questions that can be answered correctly at the time the test is taken. On the other hand, if it is presumed that a person's state of knowledge is variable and inconstant, even during very short intervals of time, then it is reasonable to think of the number of questions answered correctly on a test as only one reading of a random variable; and a probability of occurrence is associated with each different score that can be observed for the random variable. In this context, the notion of true score as a mean or expected value seems both valid and plausible.

Which conception of true score is applicable in a situation such as that described at the beginning of the preceding paragraph is a matter of personal preference on the part of a researcher. One's preferred conception, however, has consequences for the way one thinks about measurement. In particular, it is not possible to apply reliability theory as it is developed here if the Platonic conception of true score is adopted.

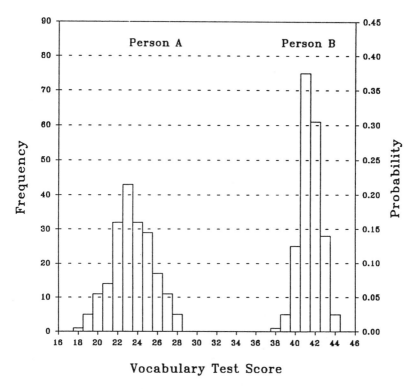

Figure 3.1. The histograms depicted for Persons A and B can be interpreted in either of two ways: (1) As frequency histograms of the scores obtained in a repeated measurement experiment, each person being tested 200 times with a 50-item vocabulary test. (2) As distributions of the probability that each different score will be obtained when the person-specific observed-score random variables for the two individuals are observed. Note that the person-specific observed-score random variable for Person A has a smaller expected value (true score) and a larger standard deviation (standard error of measurement) than those for Person B.

distributions for two persons on the 0 to 50 score scale. According to Figure 3.1, Person B will always attain a higher observed score than Person A, regardless of which values of the two random variables arise when both persons are tested. As is obvious from the figure, the expected-value true score for Person B is larger than the expected-value true score for Person A.

Error of Measurement

The concept of measurement error has been defined as the difference between an observed score and its associated true score. In symbolic form, this definition of measurement error is $e_p = x_p - \tau_p$, where x_p is an observation on the person-specific random variable X_p for person p, τ_p is the true score, and e_p is an observation on the person-specific error random variable E_p. (The person-specific random variables X_p and E_p have a functional relationship, each observation of X_p differing from the corresponding observation of E_p by the constant τ_p. More about this later.)

Although unobservable, measurement error is an appealing concept because it describes the differences, if any, among separate measurements of the same characteristic of a person. To make this idea concrete, we consider again an example involving the measurement of a physical characteristic, this time of the height of a tall building. Suppose several independent measurements of the height of the building are taken within a relatively short period of time. We presume that the height of the building is not affected by the measurement process and so is constant during the time these measurements are taken. Consequently, should measurements of the building's height differ among themselves, the presumption will be that these differences are due to variations in the measurements, not in the actual height, of the building. Thus measurement error is *not* a property of the characteristic of the object being measured; measurement error is instead a property of the measurement that is taken of the characteristic of the object.

Measurement error as conceived here is random, not systematic. To see the difference, consider measuring the height of a child. If, when a measurement is taken, the child is asked to stand on a box 2 inches high and the measurement is recorded as the distance, in inches, from the floor to the top of the child's head, then the child will appear to be taller than she really is because a *systematic* error has been made. In a repeated measurement study, if the child were to stand on the box every time a measurement of height was taken, the same systematic error would be made each time. This systematic error would affect the expected value or true score of the random variable being observed when the measurement is taken, but it would not affect what we call error of measurement. The latter entity is completely unpredictable, being either positive or negative in algebraic sign and being either relatively large or relatively small in size, but with neither the algebraic sign nor the absolute value of the error being predictable from anything known about either the child or the measuring process.

The random variable for errors of measurement has at least three properties worthy of note. The first is that it is a person-specific random variable, which, as has been noted, stands in a one-to-one relationship with the observed-score random variable for the person being measured. Consequently, the probability distribution of the person-specific random variable for errors of measurement has exactly the same *shape* as the probability distribution of the person-specific random variable for observed scores for a person. A second property is that the expected values of the person-specific error random variable and the person-specific observed-score random variable are different, with the expected value of the observed-score variable being equal to the person's true score and the expected value of the error variable being equal to zero. (The latter assertion is proven in Sidebar 3.2.) Symbolically, we write these two results as follows: $\varepsilon(X_p) = \tau_p$ and $\varepsilon(E_p) = 0$. The third property to be noted here follows from the first: The variance and standard deviation of the person-specific error random variable must be exactly the same as the variance and standard deviation of the person-specific observed-score random variable. (This follows from the fact that the distributions of observed scores and of error scores have exactly the same shape, differing only in their respective centers or means. An algebraic proof is given in Sidebar 3.3.) Symbolically, we can express this result as follows: $\sigma_{X_p}^2 = \sigma_{E_p}^2$, where $\sigma_{X_p}^2$ is the variance of the observed-score random variable and $\sigma_{E_p}^2$ is the variance of the error-score random variable.

The points of the preceding paragraph are illustrated in Figure 3.2.

Standard Error of Measurement

An important quality of a measurement is determined by the size of the error associated with it. The smaller the error, the more precise—the higher the quality of—the measurement. Of course we cannot ever know the size of the error component of a particular measurement. But we can estimate the size of the variance of the error random variable. The square root of this variance is the standard deviation that is referred to as the standard error of measurement. This is an indicator of the size of measurement errors, on average, for the observed-score random variable under study. When it is the observed-score random variable for a specific person that we are interested in, we call the standard deviation

---

Sidebar 3.2

A PROOF THAT THE EXPECTED VALUE OF THE PERSON-SPECIFIC ERROR
RANDOM VARIABLE IS 0

To see why the expected value of the error-score random variable is equal to zero,
consider the following algebraic argument:

$$\varepsilon(E_p) = \varepsilon(X_p - \tau_p) = \varepsilon(X_p) - \varepsilon(\tau_p) = \tau_p - \tau_p = 0,$$

where ε is the expected-value operator (defined in Chapter 2). To follow this
argument, note the following points:

1. $\varepsilon(E_p)$ refers to the expected value or, in everyday terms, the average of the
   theoretical distribution of errors of measurement associated with the observed
   scores in the probability distribution of the observed-score random variable X_p
   for person p.
2. The expectation operator can be distributed over the terms of the linear
   expression $(X_p - \tau_p)$, so

   $$\varepsilon(X_p - \tau_p) = \varepsilon(X_p) - \varepsilon(\tau_p).$$

3. The expected value of the observed-score random variable X_p, represented by
   $\varepsilon(X_p)$, is by definition the true score, τ_p. For a given person p, τ_p is a constant.
4. When applied to a constant such as τ_p, the expected-value operator returns the
   constant itself, so $\varepsilon(\tau_p) = \tau_p$.

---

of the error random variable the *person-specific standard error of
measurement* (PSEM). We represent this standard deviation for person
p as σ_{E_p}. This quantity should be viewed as an indicator of the size of
typical measurement errors; the larger σ_{E_p}, the less reason there is to
think an observed score lies near the true score of person p.

Figure 3.1 illustrates how the PSEM can be different for different
persons, and so can reflect differences in the precision or quality of the
measurements taken of different persons. Suppose Figure 3.1 depicts
the probability distributions governing the person-specific observed-
score random variables for measurements of the vocabulary of two
individuals. Clearly, the expected size of an error in measuring the
vocabulary of Person A is larger than the expected size of an error in
measuring the vocabulary of Person B because the standard deviation
of the error random variable for Person A is larger than that for Person B.
This illustrates the fact that different persons might well have different
PSEMs.

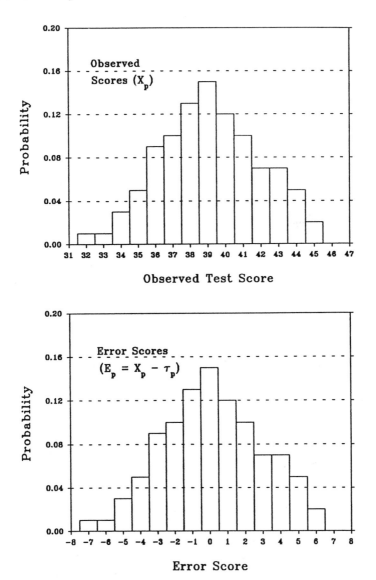

Figure 3.2. The top histogram is the probability distribution for the person-specific observed-score random variable for an individual. The bottom histogram is the probability distribution for the person-specific error random variable associated with the observed-score random variable. Note that the two random variables must have identical standard deviations but different expected values.

Sidebar 3.3

A PROOF OF THE EQUIVALENCE OF $\sigma_{X_p}^2$ AND $\sigma_{E_p}^2$

By the definition of the variance of a random variable,

$$\sigma_{X_p}^2 = \varepsilon(X_p - \mu_{X_p})^2, \qquad (3.3.1)$$

where subscript p denotes the person and X_p denotes the random variable observed whenever a characteristic of the person is measured by a particular measuring process. According to the fundamental axiom of classical reliability theory, the person-specific random variables X_p and E_p are related as follows:

$$X_p = \tau_p + E_p ,$$

which implies that

$$\mu_{X_p} \equiv \varepsilon(X_p) = \varepsilon(\tau_p - E_p) = \varepsilon(\tau_p) - \varepsilon(E_p) = \tau_p - 0 = \tau_p .$$

Substituting in Equation 3.3.1,

$$\sigma_{X_p}^2 = \varepsilon[(\tau_p + E_p) - \tau_p]^2 = \varepsilon(E_p)^2 .$$

Recalling again the definition of variance for a random variable and also the fact that $\mu_{E_p} = \varepsilon(E_p) = 0$, we have

$$\varepsilon(E_p - \mu_{E_p})^2 = \varepsilon(E_p)^2 = \sigma_{E_p}^2 ,$$

which is the result to be demonstrated.

It should be noted that the PSEM is the same as the standard deviation of the observed-score random variable for the person. This fact is demonstrated visually in Figure 3.2 and algebraically in Sidebar 3.3.

Measuring More Than One Person

To this point, we have concentrated on the measurement of just one person. Usually, however, we are interested in many different persons, and each is tested only once. The resulting measurements may be displayed as a frequency distribution, also referred to as the distribution of observed scores. A frequency distribution of the scores obtained by

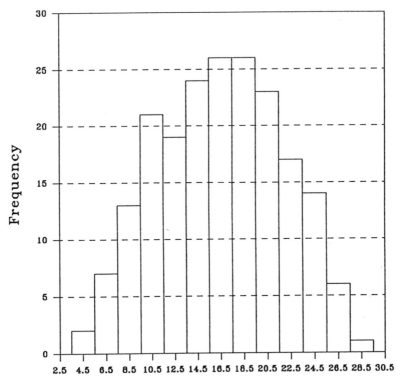

Mathematics Test Score

Figure 3.3. A Frequency Histogram of the Scores of 199 Eighth-Grade Students on a 30-Item Test of Mathematics. The variation in these scores, according to reliability theory, is due to differences in true mathematics ability plus the random errors of measurement that affect the observed scores.

199 eighth-grade students on a 30-item test of mathematics is displayed in Figure 3.3.

According to classical reliability theory, every observed measurement is viewed as the sum of a true score and an error score. Thus the variation seen in a distribution of observed scores, such as that depicted in Figure 3.3, derives from two sources: (1) variation in the true scores of the eighth-grade students and (2) variation in the errors of measurement attached to the true scores. The variation in true scores reflects real differences among persons on the characteristic being measured. Just as we expect different table tops to differ in length, we also expect students to differ in true ability or knowledge. To the extent that this expectation is valid, true scores will vary from one person to the next, and this variation will be reflected in different observed scores. (If there were no errors of measurement, the observed-score distribution for a group of persons would be identical to the true-score distribution for the group.) But how will the presence of errors of measurement affect the distribution of observed scores? Consider the following argument.

We imagine that a person-specific observed-score random variable is associated with each person in the population; this is the variable we presume is observed each time we measure a person on the characteristic under study. When each person in the population has been measured only once, we imagine that exactly one observation has been taken on the corresponding person-specific observed-score random variable for each person. The resulting observed scores are larger than the associated true scores for some persons, but smaller than the true scores for others; they lie relatively far from the true scores for some persons, but relatively near for others. Most important, there is no way to predict from anything known about a person, including the individual's true score, whether an error of measurement for the person will be positive or negative, relatively large or relatively small. This line of thinking implies that errors of measurement are uncorrelated with true scores. Inasmuch as measurement errors are combined with true scores to form the observed scores, it follows that the variance of observed scores must be larger than the variance of true scores. True scores have one source of variation, namely real differences among persons on the characteristic being measured. Observed scores reflect two sources of variation: real differences among persons on the characteristic being measured and random variation due to errors of measurement.

Implications

Let us now explore some of the implications of the conception of measurement advanced to this point. The process of measuring a characteristic of the members of a group can be imagined to define a new random variable, which is a composite of two separate random processes: (1) The individuals who are measured are presumed to have been chosen at random from a population of persons, and (2) the measurement obtained for each individual is viewed as an observation on the

---

Sidebar 3.4

A PROOF THAT $\mu_E = \varepsilon_p(E) = 0$

In the expression $\varepsilon_p(E)$, ε_p represents the operation of taking the expected value of the error random variable E over the population of persons, individual members of which are identified by the subscript p ($p = 1, 2, 3, \ldots$).

E is a random variable defined in the following way. A person, say person p, is chosen at random from the population, and the characteristic of interest is measured for that person. The act of taking the latter measurement constitutes making an observation of the person-specific random variable X_p or, equivalently, of the person-specific error random variable E_p. In Sidebar 3.2 it was shown that the expected value of the person-specific error random variable E_p is 0, that is, $\varepsilon(E_p) = 0$. Clearly, the expected value of the person-specific error random variable E_p is 0 regardless of which person p is selected at random from the population. Thus the expected value of the random variable E is the expected value, over the population of persons, of the expected values of the person-specific error random variables for every person in the population. That this expected value of an expected value must be zero is shown in the following expression:

$$\varepsilon_p(E) = \varepsilon_p[\varepsilon(E_p)] = \varepsilon_p(0) = 0.$$

---

person-specific random variable, defined earlier in this chapter as X_p. This composite random variable, say X, has an expected value or arithmetic mean, say μ_X, and a variance, say σ_X^2. (The reader is reminded that this mean and variance are *not* the mean and variance of the person-specific random variable we imagine is observed whenever an individual is measured.) In direct association with this observed-score random variable X are two other random variables: one for true scores, say T, with mean μ_T and variance σ_T^2, and another for errors of measurement, say E, with mean μ_E and variance σ_E^2. In fact, these observed, true, and error random variables are related as follows:

$$X = T + E. \tag{3.2}$$

It is possible to show for the theory just advanced (see Sidebar 3.4) that the expected value of the error random variable E is $\mu_E = 0$, in which case the expected value of the observed-score random variable X and the true-score random variable T are equal:

$$\mu_X = \mu_T. \tag{3.3}$$

Sidebar 3.5

A PROOF THAT THE COVARIANCE OF THE TRUE-SCORE RANDOM VARIABLE
T AND THE ERROR RANDOM VARIABLE E IS 0

Consider a scatterplot of error scores versus true scores, as in Figure "Sidebar 3.5." In constructing this plot, consider, first, all persons with a particular true score, say $T = \tau_A$. (Note that τ_A is an observation on T, the true-score random variable for the population at large.) The expected value of the errors of measurement for all the persons in this group is 0 because the expected value of the error of measurement for each person's observed score is 0 (by the argument advanced in Sidebar 3.4). In fact, the expected value of the errors of measurement for all persons with a different true score, say $T = \tau_B$, is also 0 by the same argument. This means that the linear regression of errors of measurement on true scores must have an expected slope coefficient, say $\beta_{E.T}$, of 0. This slope coefficient is related to the standard deviations of the random variables T and E and the correlation between random variables T and E as follows:

$$\beta_{E.T} = \left(\frac{\sigma_E}{\sigma_T}\right)\rho_{TE}$$

where $\beta_{E.T}$ is the slope of the linear regression of E on T, σ_E and σ_T are the standard deviations of the random variables E and T, respectively, and ρ_{TE} is the coefficient of correlation between E and T.

Now, if $\beta_{E.T} = 0$, then either $(\sigma_E/\sigma_T) = 0$ or $\rho_{TE} = 0$. We assume σ_T and σ_E are not zero, for to do otherwise produces a situation of trivial interest. (If σ_T were 0, then the random variable T would have the same value for every person selected from the population; if σ_E were 0, all observed measurements would be free of error; both are unlikely possibilities.) It follows, therefore, that ρ_{TE} must be 0, and, because $\rho_{TE} = (\sigma_{TE}/\sigma_T\sigma_E)$, that $\sigma_{TE} = 0$.

Also, it is possible to show (see Sidebar 3.5) that the covariance of the true-score and error-score random variables, σ_{TE}, is zero. This latter result, which follows intuitively from the idea that the sizes and algebraic signs of the errors of measurement cannot be predicted from the true-score components of observations on the random variable X, leads to an important result:

$$\sigma_X^2 = \sigma_T^2 + \sigma_E^2 , \tag{3.4}$$

which is to say, the variance of the observed-score random variable X is the simple sum of the variance of the associated true-score random variable T and the variance of the associated error-score random variable E.

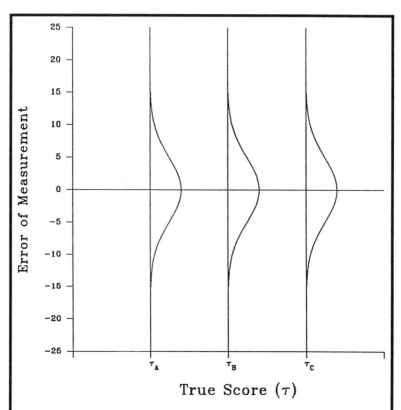

Figure "Sidebar 3.5." A Plot of the Distributions of Errors of Measurement for Each of Three Observed Scores, τ_A, τ_B, and τ_C.

NOTE: The expected value of each distribution is 0, regardless of the value of the true score. Thus, the regression of errors of measurement E on true score T over all possible values of τ will be linear, with slope coefficient $\beta_{E.T}$ of 0. This implies that the coefficient of correlation ρ_{ET} is also 0. (The standard error of measurement in this example is assumed to be 5 for all persons in the population, a convenient, but unnecessary assumption.) Note that each of the distributions depicted in this figure is a conditional distribution, that is, each is a distribution of error for the condition that variable T is fixed at some value $T = \tau$.

The results presented in Equations 3.2, 3.3, and 3.4 follow from the way the concepts of true score and error of measurement have been defined. Consequently, classical reliability theory is said to rest on *weak* assumptions. The concepts of true score and error of measurement hold, as defined, for any measuring situation encountered in social science, and no empirical test can be devised to prove the theory inapplicable for a measure.[2]

Expected Results and Sample Results

Many of the results of classical reliability theory have been derived as expectations that hold for random variables. These results can be expected to hold only approximately for samples of measurements. For example, Equation 3.4 sets forth an *expected* relationship among the variances of the random variables X, T, and E. This expected relationship is unlikely to hold exactly for the measurements obtained from a sample of examinees. In a sample, the correlation between true scores and errors of measurement is unlikely to be exactly zero, yet this expectation underlies the derivation of Equation 3.4. Still, if the sample is relatively large, perhaps 100 persons or more, the expectation stated in Equation 3.4 may be satisfied reasonably well in the sample data.

Equations setting forth expected relationships among parameters of random variables can be adapted for use with samples by substituting sample estimates for the unknown parameters. For example, an unbiased estimate of the variance of the observed-score random variable X, say σ_X^2, can be obtained from sample data by dividing the sum of squared deviations of observed scores X from the sample mean $\bar{X}$ by $(N - 1)$, where N is the sample size. Corresponding equations for sample estimates of the true-score and error variances of the random variables T and E can be defined, although we require the developments considered in Chapter 5 before we can actually obtain numerical estimates of these quantities.

Further Consideration of True-Score and Error Variances

The variance of the true-score random variable T is symbolized as σ_T^2. Because it is a variance, σ_T^2 cannot, by definition, be negative, although it could be zero. If the latter were true, all persons chosen for measurement would be observed to have the same true score.

The variance of the random variable for errors of measurement, namely E, is symbolized σ_E^2. This quantity, it must be reiterated, does not refer to the variance of the person-specific random variable E_p of a single individual p in the population. Instead, σ_E^2 is the expected value of the variance $\sigma_{E_p}^2$ of the error random variable E_p (see Sidebar 3.6). This relationship can be expressed in the following way:

$$\sigma_E^2 = \varepsilon_p[\sigma_{E_p}^2]. \qquad (3.5)$$

Sidebar 3.6

RELATING THE VARIANCES OF THE OBSERVED-SCORE, TRUE-SCORE, AND
ERROR RANDOM VARIABLES, X, T, AND E

There are two sources of the variation in random variable X, one due to differences among the examinees—each person in the population has a true score on the measure of the characteristic, and, except in unusual situations not considered here, true scores vary from person to person—and the other due to the person-specific random variable for each person who is measured. According to a fundamental theorem of statistics,

$$\sigma_X^2 = \sigma_p^2[\varepsilon(X_p)] + \varepsilon_p[\sigma_{X_p}^2], \qquad (3.6.1)$$

where $\varepsilon(X_p) \equiv \tau_p$ is, as before, the expected value or true score of the person-specific random variable that is observed whenever the characteristic of person p is measured, and $\sigma_{X_p}^2$ is the variance of this random variable. Thus the first term on the right-hand side of Equation 3.6.1 is the variance of the true-score random variable T, that is, σ_T^2, and the second term is the expected value over the population of persons of the variances of the person-specific random variable X_p. Recall (Sidebar 3.3) that for person p,

$$\sigma_{X_p}^2 = \sigma_{E_p}^2 .$$

Consequently, the second term of Equation 3.6.1 may be written as $\varepsilon_p[\sigma_{E_p}^2]$, which is the average over the population of persons of the distribution of error variances for those persons and has been symbolized as σ_E^2. Thus Equation 3.6.1 translates into the equation

$$\sigma_X^2 = \sigma_T^2 + \sigma_E^2 .$$

This quantity too must be nonnegative, although it would be zero if all measurements were made without error. (In the latter event, the person-specific observed-score random variable X_p and its derivative, the person-specific error random variable E_p, would have zero variance for every person p.)

Summary

A theoretical framework for reliability was constructed by considering first the process of measuring a characteristic of a single person, and then applying the concepts so developed to the more complicated matter of measuring the characteristic in more than one individual. At the heart of this development are three random variables, the observed-score, true-score, and error-score variables. The relationships among these variables, and among the expected values and variances of these variables, were derived and are expressed in Equations 3.2, 3.3, and 3.4. These consist of (1) the fundamental equation of reliability theory, that an observed score is the sum of a true-score component and an error-score component; (2) the result that the expected value of the error random variable is zero, which implies that the expected values of the observed-score and true-score random variables are equal; and (3) the result that the variance of the observed-score variable is the simple sum of the variances of the true-score and error-score random variables. In the process of deriving the latter result, it was necessary to evaluate the covariance of the true-score and error-score random variables; this covariance was shown to be zero. The immediate challenge is to build on these fundamental ideas to define the concept of reliability.

Exercises

3.1. Suppose a test is composed of 10 questions, and answers to the questions are scored 1 for correct, 0 for incorrect. Consider the following numbers: 8; 3.6; 10; 1.111. Indicate which, if any, of these numbers is a possible observed score on the test, and state why you think so. Now indicate which, if any, could be a true score. An error score.

3.2. What is meant by "Platonic true score"? Give an example different from the one given in Chapter 3.

3.3. (i) Give a general algebraic expression to describe the relative magnitudes of observed-score variance and true-score variance for the measurements obtained on a group of examinees.

(ii) Is there a general expression that describes the relative magnitudes, for the same set of measurements, of the variances of true scores and error scores? If yes, what is it? If no, why not?

3.4. The essays of two examinees are rated on a 10-point scale by raters drawn at random from a population of raters. After the ratings have been made by a large number of raters, the essay of the first examinee is found to have received an equal number of each of the ratings 2, 3, and 4, whereas the essay of the second examinee received an equal number of each of the ratings 5, 6, 7, 8, and 9. What do these results indicate about the quality of the essays written by the two examinees? About the errors incurred in marking the two essays?

Notes

1. A *linear combination* of a set of terms—numbers or symbols representing variables or constants—is an algebraic expression in which the terms on the right-hand side of the expression are connected by the operators for addition "+" or subtraction "−" or, in combinations of more than two terms, by a sequence of these operators. For example, the observed scores on two tests for person p might be represented as x_{1p} and x_{2p}. The difference between these scores, say $y_p = x_{1p} - x_{2p}$, is a linear combination. So too is the following expression: $y_p = (\tau_{1p} + e_{1p}) - (\tau_{2p} + e_{2p}) = \tau_{1p} + e_{1p} - \tau_{2p} - e_{2p}$, where τ_{ip} is the true score of person p on test i, $i = 1, 2$, and e_{ip} is the error incurred when the measurement $X_{ip} = x_{ip}$ was obtained for person p.

2. An additional technical assumption needs to be satisfied for the theory to apply—the variances of the random variables X, T, and E must be finite. This assumption will be met if the scale of measurement is finite, that is, if the scale of measurement is limited to only a small portion of the real number line. This restriction is realistic for educational and psychological tests, and for most, if not all, other measuring processes encountered in the social sciences.

4

Reliability

At the beginning of this book, reliability was discussed in terms of consistency, whether of the performance of machines, the behavior of persons, or the measurements of characteristics of objects or persons. The task ahead is to add meaning to the notion of reliability, using the theoretical concepts developed thus far.

Reliability Coefficient

The reliability coefficient, symbolized as ρ_X^2, is defined as the ratio of true-score variance, σ_T^2, to observed-score variance, σ_X^2. (Sidebar 4.1 contains a discussion of the reliability coefficient from which it can be seen why this coefficient is written as ρ_X^2, not as ρ_X.) The observed-score variance may be expressed as the sum of the true-score and error-score variances, that is, as $\sigma_X^2 = \sigma_T^2 + \sigma_E^2$. Consequently, ρ_X^2 can be written in equation form as follows:

$$\rho_X^2 = \frac{\sigma_T^2}{\sigma_X^2}$$

$$= \frac{\sigma_T^2}{\sigma_T^2 + \sigma_E^2}. \tag{4.1}$$

The variances σ_T^2 and σ_E^2 are nonnegative quantities, and we assume at least one of these variances is greater than zero, implying that the observed-score variance is greater than zero. Consequently, ρ_X^2 has the desirable quality of being bounded below by zero and above by one. The reliability coefficient will be near its lower bound, zero, when the variance of observed scores is almost totally due to error-score variance and the true scores of the objects of measurement are very nearly all the same (e.g., all tables are of nearly the same length; all students possess nearly the same ability to spell words). But, ρ_X^2 will be near the upper bound of one when the variance of observed scores is nearly all due to differences among true scores and the specific observed-score random variable for each object of measurement has almost no variance, which is to say measurements are, relatively speaking, error free. Reliability coefficients near one reflect a preponderance of true-score variance in the measurements, hence such coefficients mark measurements of relatively high precision. Coefficients near zero reflect a large proportion of error-score variance in the measurements; such measurements are said to possess relatively low precision.

Just how high a reliability coefficient must be to be deemed acceptable depends on a number of considerations, not the least of which is the size of the reliability coefficients typically realized for measures of a particular kind. Well-constructed, objectively scored tests of cognitive ability and scholastic achievement can routinely produce test scores for heterogeneous groups of examinees for which the coefficient of reliability is 0.8 or larger. The reliability coefficients for scores on subjectively scored tests of ability and achievement and for measures of typical performance (e.g., personality inventories) are often less than 0.8, sometimes substantially less. Other factors affecting the reliability coefficient are considered in Chapter 7.

The reliability coefficient ρ_X^2, as developed to this point, is a completely abstract quantity. No means has yet been proposed in this book for estimating the true-score variance of a set of measurements. This important matter is dealt with in subsequent chapters.

Uses of the Reliability Coefficient

Reliability coefficients serve several useful purposes. For one, the reliability coefficient for the measurements of a group of examinees, together with the observed-score standard deviation of the measurements, can be used to obtain an estimate of the standard error of measurement (see Sidebar 4.2). The standard error of measurement, in turn, can be used to calculate a confidence interval for a test-taker's true score (see Sidebar 4.3), and, more generally, it provides an impression of the variability that would be expected in a person's observed scores were it possible to measure the person repeatedly, as in the hypothetical repeated measurement experiment described earlier.

Sidebar 4.1

WHY IS THE SYMBOL FOR THE RELIABILITY COEFFICIENT ρ_X^2, NOT ρ_X?

The coefficient of reliability can be defined as the squared coefficient of correlation between observed scores and true scores, that is, as ρ_{XT}^2 (Lord & Novick, 1968, p. 61). To see that this definition is equivalent to the definition of reliability as the ratio of true-score to observed-score variance under the assumptions we have made, consider the correlation coefficient ρ_{XT}. By the definition of a correlation coefficient, we may write

$$\rho_{XT} = \frac{\sigma_{XT}}{\sigma_X \sigma_T}.$$

But $\sigma_{XT} = \sigma_{(T+E)T} = \sigma_{TT} + \sigma_{ET} = \sigma_T^2$, because the expected covariance of errors of measurement E with true scores T (i.e., σ_{ET}) is zero, as shown in the previous chapter. So

$$\rho_{XT} = \frac{\sigma_T^2}{\sigma_X \sigma_T} = \frac{\sigma_T}{\sigma_X}.$$

This quantity is referred to as the *index of reliability* (Lord & Novick, 1968, p. 61). The fact that reliability can be defined as a squared coefficient of correlation is indicated in the symbol adopted here for the reliability coefficient, namely ρ_X^2.

Another use of the reliability coefficient is in correcting coefficients of correlation for the attenuation—the reduction in absolute value—they suffer due to the effect of errors in the measurements of one or the other or both of the variables that were correlated. The coefficient of correlation[1] between observed scores on two variables will be no larger, and in general it will be smaller, in absolute magnitude than the coefficient between the corresponding true scores on the variables. The reason is that random errors of measurement, when present, make the observed scores on a variable less predictable from another variable than are their associated true scores. The coefficient of correlation between two true-score random variables is related to the coefficient of correlation between the associated observed-score random variables as follows:

$$\rho_{T_X T_Y} = \frac{\rho_{XY}}{\rho_{XT_X} \rho_{YT_Y}}, \tag{4.2}$$

Sidebar 4.2

ESTIMATING THE STANDARD ERROR OF MEASUREMENT

To see how an estimate might be obtained of the standard error of measurement, note that the equation

$$\sigma_X^2 = \sigma_T^2 + \sigma_E^2$$

implies that

$$\sigma_E^2 = \sigma_X^2 - \sigma_T^2 . \qquad (4.2.1)$$

Also, manipulation of Equation 4.1 gives the result

$$\sigma_T^2 = \sigma_X^2 \rho_X^2 ,$$

which, when substituted in Equation 4.2.1, yields an expression for the variance of errors of measurement in terms of the variance and coefficient of reliability of the observed scores:

$$\sigma_E^2 = \sigma_X^2 - \sigma_X^2 \rho_X^2$$

$$= \sigma_X^2 (1 - \rho_X^2) .$$

The standard error of measurement then is

$$\sigma_E = \sigma_X \sqrt{1 - \rho_X^2} . \qquad (4.2.2)$$

An estimate of σ_E can be obtained by substituting sample estimates of σ_X and ρ_X^2 in Equation 4.2.2 to yield

$$\hat{\sigma}_E = \hat{\sigma}_X \sqrt{1 - \hat{\rho}_X^2} . \qquad (4.2.3)$$

So, for example, if the estimate $\hat{\sigma}_X$ was 15 and the estimate $\hat{\rho}_X^2$ was 0.91, the estimated standard error of measurement would be $15\sqrt{0.09}$ or 4.5.

Granted, the standard error of measurement (SEM) that is estimated using the reliability coefficient is not the one we would prefer to have. This SEM may be interpreted as the expected value or arithmetic mean of the person-specific standard errors of measurement (PSEMs) that could be estimated were it possible to conduct the repeated-measurement experiment on every examinee selected for measurement. So the SEM of Equation 4.2.3 does not necessarily equal the magnitude of the PSEM for any one test-taker. The saving grace of Equation 4.2.3 is that it is easy to use and it provides an indication, however unrepresentative it may be for particular individuals, of the variability in test scores that is due to measurement error. Other ways of estimating the standard error of measurement for the test scores of individual examinees are considered in Chapter 8.

Sidebar 4.3
OBTAINING A CONFIDENCE INTERVAL FOR A TRUE SCORE

The rationale underlying the procedure for estimating a confidence interval for an examinee's true score is identical to that used in statistics for estimating a confidence interval for the population mean (see, e.g., Marascuilo & Serlin, 1988, pp. 283-288). It is assumed that observations on an examinee's person-specific random variable X_p are distributed normally, with a mean of τ_p and a standard deviation of $\sigma_{E_p}^2$. Given an observed score for the examinee of $X_p = x_p$, and setting the standard deviation $\sigma_{E_p}^2$ equal to the estimated group standard error of measurement $\hat{\sigma}_E$, a 68% confidence interval for the examinee's true score is $x_p \pm \hat{\sigma}_E$. If $x_p = 110$ and $\hat{\sigma}_E = 4.5$, then a 68% confidence interval for the person's true score is [105.5, 114.5].

It might seem odd that a 68% confidence interval was constructed here, whereas in statistics, if we take the example of the arithmetic mean, it is common to work with 90% or 95% or even 99% confidence intervals. A reason lies in the fact that the standard error of the mean is considerably smaller than the standard error of individual test scores. For the interpretation of individual test scores, 68% confidence is often viewed as sufficient.

---

where $\rho_{T_X T_Y}$ is the coefficient of correlation between the true-score random variables T_X and T_Y; ρ_{XY} is the coefficient of correlation between observed-score random variables X and Y; and ρ_{XT_X} and ρ_{YT_Y} are the square roots of the coefficients of reliability, ρ_X^2 and ρ_Y^2, for random variables X and Y, respectively. (A proof of Equation 4.2 is provided in Sidebar 4.4.) So, for example, if the correlation between observed scores on two variables is 0.6, and the coefficient of reliability for each of the variables is 0.75, the estimated coefficient of correlation between true scores on the variables is

$$\rho_{T_X T_Y} = \frac{\rho_{XY}}{\rho_{XT_X}\rho_{YT_Y}} = \frac{0.6}{\sqrt{0.75 \times 0.75}} = 0.8 .$$

We see that whereas only 36% [$100\rho_{XY}^2\% = 100(.6)^2\% = 36\%$] of the variance in observed scores of Y can be accounted for in terms of the variation in observed scores in X, the larger amount of 64% [$100\rho_{T_X T_Y}^2\% = 100(.8)^2\% = 64\%$] of the variance in true scores in Y can be accounted for from variation in true scores in X.

If the coefficient of correlation between observed scores on two random variables is small, an estimate of the coefficient of correlation between true scores on the two variables will help us interpret the observed-score coefficient. One possibility is that the observed-score correlation coeffi-

---

Sidebar 4.4

A PROOF OF THE CORRECTION FOR ATTENUATION (EQUATION 4.2)

The objective here is to show the relationship between $\rho_{T_X T_Y}$, the coefficient of correlation between the true-score random variables T_X and T_Y, and ρ_{XY}, the coefficient of correlation between observed-score random variables X and Y. From the definition of a correlation coefficient we can write the following expression:

$$\rho_{T_X T_Y} = \frac{\sigma_{T_X T_Y}}{\sigma_{T_X} \sigma_{T_Y}}$$

Looking ahead, it will be demonstrated in Sidebar 5.1 that $\sigma_{T_X T_Y} = \sigma_{XY}$. Also, from the definition of the reliability coefficient and developments presented in Sidebar 4.1, $\sigma_{T_X} = \sigma_X \sqrt{\rho_X^2} = \sigma_X \rho_{XT_X}$. Similarly, $\sigma_{T_Y} = \sigma_Y \sqrt{\rho_Y^2} = \sigma_Y \rho_{YT_Y}$. Consequently, we have

$$\rho_{T_X T_Y} = \frac{\sigma_{XY}}{\sigma_X \rho_{XT_X} \sigma_Y \rho_{YT_Y}} \tag{4.4.1}$$

$$= \left(\frac{\sigma_{XY}}{\sigma_X \sigma_Y} \right) \left(\frac{1}{\rho_{XT_X} \rho_{YT_Y}} \right)$$

$$= \frac{\rho_{XY}}{\rho_{XT_X} \rho_{YT_Y}},$$

the result to be demonstrated. Inasmuch as ρ_{XT_X} and ρ_{YT_Y} are positive numbers—they are the square roots of reliability coefficients, which are not negative by definition—and are at most equal to 1, the denominator of the right-hand side of Equation 4.4.1 is in general less than 1. Hence, the true-score correlation coefficient $\rho_{T_X T_Y}$ is never smaller, and is almost always larger in absolute value than the observed-score correlation coefficient ρ_{XY}.

---

cient is small because the variables are truly unrelated, which would be the case if the corrected (for unreliability) correlation coefficient differed very little from the uncorrected coefficient. An alternative possibility is that the observed-score correlation coefficient is small principally due to errors in the measurements of both variables. In the latter case, the corrected coefficient would be much nearer to 1 or −1. The corrected coefficient indicates how well we could expect to predict one variable from the other were we to improve the reliability of the measurements involved to the point where the reliability coefficients were very nearly 1.

A third use for reliability coefficients is in comparing the relative merits of two or more instruments being considered for the same application (career counseling, assessment of educational achievement, etc.). This type of comparison is difficult, for it involves factors other than reliability, such as usability and validity. In particular, if the scores on two tests are not equally valid for the purpose for which the tests are being considered, then reliability is very likely to be a minor consideration. But the empirical evidence needed to judge whether or not two tests measure precisely the same thing is rarely reported, so it is usually not possible to ascertain with any degree of precision whether the scores on two different tests are equally valid for a given purpose. Frequently, then, a comparison must be made of two instruments on the basis of available information, and this comparison can be informed by coefficients of reliability.

Summary

At the beginning of this chapter, we defined the reliability coefficient as the ratio of true-score variance to observed-score variance, and showed this coefficient to be a number that ranges in value from 0 for total lack of reliability (in the sense that all of the observed-score variance can be attributed to error variance) to 1 for total reliability (in the sense that all of the observed-score variance can be ascribed to variation in the true scores). Three uses for the reliability coefficient were then considered: (1) in estimating the standard error of measurement, which can be used to establish confidence intervals for true scores; (2) in correcting coefficients of correlation for attenuation due to unreliability in measuring the variables correlated; and (3) in describing and evaluating the quality of measures. Next, we need to find a practical way of estimating both the reliability coefficient and the standard error of measurement.

Exercises

4.1. The true-score variance for a test random variable is known to be 190 and the observed-score variance is known to be 225. What is the reliability of test scores for this variable?

4.2. If the standard error of measurement for a test is 4.5, and the corresponding standard deviation of true scores is 10, what is the coefficient of reliability?

4.3. The PSEM for an examinee on a test is 5. Calculate a 68% confidence interval for the examinee's true score, given that his or her observed score was 85 out of a possible maximum score of 100.

4.4. Suppose a second examinee took the test described in Exercise 4.3 and achieved an observed score of 97. If the PSEM for this examinee is also 5, the 68% confidence interval yields an absurd result. What is the absurd result and how is it to be dealt with?

Note

1. The coefficient of correlation is of great interest in test theory as an indicator of validity. If we imagine being in possession of a measure of the criterion variable a test has been constructed to measure, then the coefficient of correlation between the test and the criterion variable is a measure of the extent to which the test measures what it was intended to measure. This is one way of making operational the notion of test validity.

5

Estimating the Reliability Coefficient

Developments thus far have produced a theoretical structure within which the concept of reliability has been defined. But we are still unable to compute the reliability coefficient, ρ_X^2, because we have not yet developed a way of evaluating the true-score variance, σ_T^2. It turns out, however, that if we can repeat a measurement process even once, thereby obtaining two measurements of a characteristic for a group of examinees, then, in some circumstances at least, we can estimate the reliability coefficient. The following theoretical developments show how two replicate measurements can provide this estimate.

Parallel Tests

Suppose we could build two tests of the same characteristic, such that the person-specific observed-score random variables for an individual on both instruments (1) had the same expected-value true scores and (2) had the same variances or, equivalently, the same standard errors of measurement. Suppose, moreover, that these conditions were satisfied for every person who might be tested. Formally, we can express these suppositions as follows:

$$(1) \quad \tau_{1p} = \tau_{2p} \tag{5.1}$$

and

$$(2) \quad \sigma_{E_{1p}}^2 = \sigma_{E_{2p}}^2 \,, \tag{5.2}$$

where τ_{1p} is the true score of person p on Test 1, τ_{2p} is the true score of person p on Test 2, $\sigma_{E_{1p}}^2$ is the variance of the person-specific error random variable for person p on Test 1, and $\sigma_{E_{2p}}^2$ is the variance of the person-specific error random variable for person p on Test 2.[1] Two tests that yield measurements satisfying the foregoing assumptions are called *parallel tests*.

The assumptions for parallel tests imply that the observed-score random variables, which are defined by testing randomly chosen individuals from a population with each of two parallel tests, will possess the following characteristics:

1. The expected values of the observed-score random variables for parallel tests will be the same, that is

$$\varepsilon(X_1) = \mu_{X_1} = \mu_{X_2} = \varepsilon(X_2) . \tag{5.3}$$

This follows from the twin facts

   i. that $\mu_{E_1} = \mu_{E_2} = 0$, because of the way error of measurement is defined for any test, including ones that are parallel (see Sidebar 3.2), and
   ii. that $\mu_{T_1} = \mu_{T_2}$, because of the assumption expressed in Equation 5.1. (Different persons are very likely to have different true scores on a test, but if every person who might be sampled and tested has the same true score on each of two parallel tests, then the expected values over persons of the true-score random variables for the two tests must be equal.)

Inasmuch as the expected value of the *observed*-score random variable for a test is equal to the expected value of the *true*-score random variable for the test, we can form the following chain of equivalent expected values for parallel tests:

$$\mu_{X_1} = \mu_{T_1} = \mu_{T_2} = \mu_{X_2} .$$

2. The variance of the observed-score random variable for a test will be the same as the variance of the observed-score random variable for a parallel test, that is,

$$\sigma_{X_1}^2 = \sigma_{X_2}^2 . \tag{5.4}$$

This follows from Equation 3.4 ($\sigma_X^2 = \sigma_T^2 + \sigma_E^2$) with the addition of two observations:

   i. By the assumption expressed in Equation 5.1, that $\tau_{1p} = \tau_{2p}$, we see that $\sigma_{T_1}^2 = \sigma_{T_2}^2$; the reason is that each person who could be chosen for testing has the same true score on both tests, so all moments, including the variance, of the true-score random variable of one of the tests must equal the corresponding moments of the true-score random variable of the other test. (Return to Chapter 2, if necessary, to review the definition of *moments of a random variable.*)

   ii. By the assumption expressed in Equation 5.2, namely that $\sigma_{E_{1p}}^2 = \sigma_{E_{2p}}^2$, we see that

$$\sigma_{E_1}^2 = \varepsilon_p[\sigma_{E_{1p}}^2] = \varepsilon_p[\sigma_{E_{2p}}^2] = \sigma_{E_2}^2 . \tag{5.5}$$

{If each person has the same person-specific standard error of measurement for each test, then the expected value over persons of the squared PSEM, namely $\varepsilon_p[\sigma_{E_{ip}}^2]$, ($i = 1$ or 2), will be the same for each parallel test (refer again to Equation 3.4).}

3. The covariance of the observed-score random variable for a test and the observed-score random variable for some other quantitative characteristic (e.g., the covariance between scores on a test of vocabulary and average grades in the final year of high school) will equal the covariance of the observed-score random variable for a parallel test (e.g., a parallel test of vocabulary) and the variable for the other quantitative characteristic. Expressed in equation form,

$$\sigma_{X_1 Y} = \sigma_{X_2 Y} , \tag{5.6}$$

where X_1 and X_2 are the observed-score random variables for the parallel tests and Y is the other quantitative characteristic of interest. Equation 5.6 follows from two assumptions:

   i. The assumption of equal true scores, stated in Equation 5.1 as $\tau_{1p} = \tau_{2p}$.

   ii. The assumption that the error random variables E_{X_1}, E_{X_2}, and E_Y, which, respectively, are parts of the observed-score random variables $X_1, X_2,$ and Y, each has zero covariance with either of the other two error random variables and zero covariance with any one of the three true-score random variables T_{X_1}, T_{X_2}, and T_Y. This assumption implies that the covariance of the observed-score random variables X_1 (or X_2) and Y depends only on the covariance of the true-score random variables T_1 (or T_2) and T_Y.

(A proof of the result stated in Equation 5.6 is given in Sidebar 5.1.)

4. Variable Y in preceding Point 3 could be a third parallel test, say X_3. It follows, therefore, that for a set of three or more parallel tests, the covariance between the observed-score random variables for any pair of tests from the set must equal the covariance between the random variables for any other pair of tests from the set. Symbolically, we can state this point as follows: $\sigma_{X_1X_2} = \sigma_{X_1X_3} = \sigma_{X_2X_3} = \ldots$.

The developments presented here for two parallel tests can be extended to any number of parallel tests. The observed-score or true-score random variables for all tests that are parallel should have equal expected values, equal variances, and equal covariances with the observed-score or true-score random variables for the measure of any other characteristic, say Y. These results further imply that the *coefficient of correlation* between the observed-score or true-score random variable for any test from a set of parallel tests and the observed-score or true-score random variable for another measure should be equal to the coefficient of correlation between the observed-score or true-score random variable for any other test in the set of parallel instruments and the observed-score or true-score random variable for the other measure. This result is expressed algebraically as follows:

$$\rho_{X_1Y} = \rho_{X_2Y} = \rho_{X_3Y} = \ldots, \text{ and } \rho_{T_1T_Y} = \rho_{T_2T_Y} = \rho_{T_3T_Y} = \ldots,$$

where X_1, X_2, X_3, . . . are the observed-score random variables for parallel tests and Y is the observed-score random variable for the other measure; likewise, T_1, T_2, T_3, . . . are the true-score random variables for the parallel tests and T_Y is the true-score random variable for the other measure.

A numerical illustration of the results that can be expected for parallel measures is provided in Table 5.1. Note especially which numbers are equal and which are different.

Sidebar 5.1

SOME ASSUMPTIONS AND CONSEQUENCES PERTAINING TO COVARIANCES
OF PARALLEL TESTS

An assumption made for any two tests administered independently to the examinees in a population is that the error random variable for either test has zero
covariance with the error random variable for the other test, and that the error random
variable for either test has zero covariance with the true-score random variable for
the other test. For two parallel tests, these assumptions can be stated as follows:

$$\sigma_{E_1 E_2} = 0 \qquad\qquad (5.1.1)$$

and

$$\sigma_{T_1 E_2} = \sigma_{T_2 E_1} = 0 \, , \qquad\qquad (5.1.2)$$

where T_1 and E_1 are the true-score and error random variables for parallel test 1 and
T_2 and E_2 are the true-score and error random variables for parallel test 2. (We do
not have to assume that $\sigma_{T_1 E_1} = \sigma_{T_2 E_2} = 0$ because the true-score and error-score
variables for a test have been constructed to have zero covariances. This fact was
demonstrated in Sidebar 3.5.) It follows from the assumptions expressed in Equations
5.1.1 and 5.1.2 that

$$\sigma_{X_1 X_2} = \sigma_{[(T_1 + E_1)(T_2 + E_2)]}$$

$$= \sigma_{T_1 T_2} + \sigma_{T_1 E_2} + \sigma_{T_2 E_1} + \sigma_{E_1 E_2}$$

Reliability as a Correlation Coefficient

Parallel tests are important because they make it possible to estimate
the coefficient of reliability. It is shown in this section that the coefficient of correlation between parallel measures is equal to the reliability
coefficient, which was defined in Chapter 4 as the proportion of observed-score variance that is true-score variance.

Recall that it was shown in Sidebar 5.1 (Equation 5.1.3), that

$$\sigma_{X_1 X_2} = \sigma_{T_1 T_2} \, . \qquad\qquad (5.7)$$

The right-hand side of Equation 5.7 is the covariance between the true-
score random variables of two tests. Because the tests are parallel, the true
scores for any person p on the two tests, say τ_{1p} and τ_{2p}, will be equal.

Sidebar 5.1 Continued

$$= \sigma_{T_1 T_2} . \qquad (5.1.3)$$

In other words, under the assumptions stated in Equations 5.1.1 and 5.1.2, the covariance between the observed-score random variables for two parallel tests is due solely to the covariance between the true-score random variables for the tests.

The result expressed in Equation 5.1.3 has been derived for the special case of parallel tests, but it holds for any pair of tests for which the assumptions of Equations 5.1.1 and 5.1.2 apply. In particular, given test variables X_1 and Y and the results of Equation 5.1.3, it follows that $\sigma_{X_1 Y} = \sigma_{T_{X_1} T_Y}$. Also, given test variables X_2 and Y, it follows that $\sigma_{X_2 Y} = \sigma_{T_{X_2} T_Y}$. If the variables X_1 and X_2 are for parallel tests, in which case $\tau_{1p} = \tau_{2p}$ for all persons p who might be chosen for testing, then

$$\sigma_{T_{X_1} T_Y} = \sigma_{T_{X_2} T_Y}$$

and

$$\sigma_{X_1 Y} = \sigma_{T_{X_1} T_Y} = \sigma_{T_{X_2} T_Y} = \sigma_{X_2 Y} . \qquad (5.1.4)$$

The result expressed in Equation 5.1.4 means that if the covariance between scores on Form 1 of an intelligence test and school grade-point average is 150, then the covariance between parallel Form 2 or 3 or 4 of the intelligence test and school grade-point average will also be 150.

Next recall what was shown in Chapter 2, that the covariance between the true-score random variables for two parallel tests, X_1 and X_2, can be expressed as follows:

$$\sigma_{T_1 T_2} = \varepsilon_p[(\tau_{1p} - \mu_{T_1})(\tau_{2p} - \mu_{T_2})] , \qquad (5.8)$$

where the expectation is over all persons who might be sampled in taking observations on the random variables. Using the fact that the true scores of person p on each of two parallel tests are equal, Equation 5.8 can be rewritten as follows:

$$\sigma_{T_1 T_2} = \varepsilon_p[(\tau_{1p} - \mu_{T_1})(\tau_{1p} - \mu_{T_1})]$$

$$= \varepsilon_p[(\tau_{1p} - \mu_{T_1})^2] . \qquad (5.9)$$

TABLE 5.1 Numerical Illustration of Equivalent Statistics for Three Parallel Tests and Another Variable

Variable Designation	Expected Values (μ)	Variances σ^2	Reliability Coefficients	Coefficients of Covariance / Correlation*			
				X_1	X_2	X_3	Y
Parallel Test 1 (X_1)	100	225	0.92	—	207	207	78
Parallel Test 2 (X_2)	100	225	0.92	0.92	—	207	78
Parallel Test 3 (X_3)	100	225	0.92	0.92	0.92	—	78
Another Variable (Y)	70	64	0.80	0.65	0.65	0.65	—

* Coefficients of covariance are above the diagonal, which is marked by dashes (—), and coefficients of correlation are below the diagonal.

The right-hand side of the second line of Equation 5.9 is an expression for the variance of random variable T_1. So, recalling Equation 5.7, we can write the following sequence of equivalent terms:

$$\sigma_{T_1 T_2} = \sigma_{T_1}^2 = \sigma_{T_2}^2 = \sigma_T^2 = \sigma_{X_1 X_2} . \tag{5.10}$$

Thus we see that the covariance between the observed-score random variables for two parallel tests is equal to the variance of the true-score random variable for either test.

Now we are ready to show that the coefficient of correlation between two parallel tests is the coefficient of reliability for either test. As noted in Chapter 2, the coefficient of correlation is defined as the covariance divided by the product of the standard deviations of the variables involved. In equation form,

$$\rho_{X_1 X_2} = \frac{\sigma_{X_1 X_2}}{\sigma_{X_1} \sigma_{X_2}} . \tag{5.11}$$

Recalling that $\sigma_{X_1} = \sigma_{X_2}$ and that $\sigma_{X_1 X_2} = \sigma_T^2$ for parallel tests, and substituting these results in Equation 5.11, we obtain the following expression:

$$\rho_{X_1 X_2} = \frac{\sigma_T^2}{\sigma_X^2} \tag{5.12}$$

$$= \rho_X^2 .$$

What Equation 5.12 indicates is this: If it is possible to build tests that are approximately parallel, then it is possible to estimate the reliability of the measurements provided by either test by correlating the scores obtained in an experiment in which both instruments are administered to the same sample of persons. We consider some of the issues involved in conducting such experiments in the next chapter. The numerical example provided in Table 5.1 indicates that the reliability of each parallel test was 0.92. This fact can be read directly from the table as a correlation coefficient between any pair of the parallel tests or calculated by dividing the covariance for any pair of the tests by the variance for any one of them.

The significance of being able to construct parallel or approximately parallel tests cannot be overemphasized. In addition to enabling us to estimate the coefficient of reliability, ρ_X^2, parallel tests provide a means of estimating the standard error of measurement. To see that this is so, take again Equation 3.4 ($\sigma_X^2 = \sigma_T^2 + \sigma_E^2$) and solve for σ_E^2. Next, take Equation 5.12 and solve for σ_T^2. Finally, put these two sets of results together as follows:

$$\sigma_E^2 = \sigma_X^2 - \sigma_T^2$$

$$= \sigma_X^2 - \sigma_X^2 \rho_{X_1 X_2}$$

$$= \sigma_X^2 (1 - \rho_{X_1 X_2}). \tag{5.13}$$

The standard error of measurement, σ_E, is the square root of the quantity on the right-hand side of Equation 5.13. Provided it is possible to construct parallel tests, the terms on the right-hand side of Equation 5.13 can be estimated from data. So, given the scores resulting from the administration of two parallel tests to a sample of persons, the variance σ_X^2 can be estimated from the distribution of scores for either parallel test, and an estimate of the reliability coefficient, $\rho_X^2 = \rho_{X_1 X_2}$, can be obtained by correlating the scores for both parallel tests. Although not indicated in Table 5.1, the standard error of measurement for any one of the parallel tests in that example is 4.24 [$= \sqrt{18} = \sqrt{225(1 - 0.92)}$].

Testing the Hypothesis of Parallel Tests

The properly skeptical reader will question whether it is possible to construct parallel tests. The hypothesis of parallel measures is a stringent one. To be deemed parallel, it is required that, on the basis of an analysis of their contents, instruments appear to measure the same characteristic. Beyond this, the instruments must produce observed scores that satisfy more or less closely the statistical criteria stated in Equations 5.3, 5.4, and 5.6. A set of measures thought to be parallel can be administered to a sample of examinees, and the hypothesis of equal expected values, the hypothesis of equal variances, and, for all possible pairs of measures, the hypothesis of equal covariances can be tested statistically. When three or more tests are included in the set of instruments thought to be parallel, the aforementioned hypotheses can be tested efficiently by means of a procedure called analysis of covariance structures (Fleishman & Benson, 1987; Jöreskog & Sörbom, 1989; Linn & Werts, 1979). This procedure, however, is not described here.

Provided the examination of a set of instruments developed to be parallel is thorough enough, the conclusion that they are *not* parallel will almost certainly be supported. In many applications, however, it may not be important even to try to get a yes or no answer to the question of parallelism for a set of tests. Instead, we may decide, after considering the available evidence—test means, test standard deviations, and test covariances—that two or more instruments are close enough to being parallel to reap the benefits of assuming they really are parallel. These benefits include the reliability coefficient and standard error of measurement that can be estimated from the scores obtained by a group of examinees on the tests.

Still, careful study might persuade us that two or more tests constructed to measure the same characteristic are not parallel. In this case, we might wish to consider one of several weaker hypotheses as models for the relationship among the observed-score random variables for the tests. Each of the three "weaker" hypotheses described in the following sections also provides a basis for estimating test reliability.

The Hypothesis of Tau-Equivalent Tests

For two tests, the defining assumptions of this hypothesis are as follows:

$$(1)\quad \tau_{1p} = \tau_{2p}, \qquad\qquad (5.14)$$

with the possibility that

$$(2) \quad \sigma^2_{E_{1p}} \neq \sigma^2_{E_{2p}}, \qquad\qquad (5.15)$$

where, as before, τ_{1p} is the true score of person p on Test 1, τ_{2p} is the true score of person p on Test 2, $\sigma^2_{E_{1p}}$ is the variance of the person-specific error random variable for person p on Test 1, and $\sigma^2_{E_{2p}}$ is the variance of the person-specific error random variable for person p on Test 2.

Note that the assumption of equal true scores, stated in Equation 5.14 for tau-equivalent tests, is identical to the assumption stated in Equation 5.1 for parallel tests. As before, this assumption implies that the observed-score random variables for two tau-equivalent tests, say X_1 and X_2, have equal means ($\mu_{X_1} = \mu_{X_2}$) and equal true-score variances ($\sigma^2_{T_1} = \sigma^2_{T_2}$). The equal-true-scores assumption implies two more important consequences:

(1) When combined with earlier assumptions—that the covariances between the error random variables and the true-score random variables for different measures are zero, that is, $\sigma_{E_1E_2} = 0$ and $\sigma_{T_1E_2} = \sigma_{T_2E_1} = 0$—the coefficient of covariance between the observed-score random variables for any pair of tau-equivalent tests will equal the variance of the true-score random variable for either test. Symbolically, $\sigma_{X_iX_j} = \sigma^2_{T_i} = \sigma^2_{T_j}$ for all $i, j = 1, 2, 3, \ldots$, with $i \neq j$.

(2) The covariance coefficient between the observed-score random variable for any one of a set of tau-equivalent measures and the observed-score random variable for the measure of another characteristic must equal the corresponding coefficient of covariance for any other tau-equivalent measure in the set. Symbolically, $\sigma_{X_iY} = \sigma_{X_jY}$ for all $i, j = 1, 2, 3, \ldots$, with $i \neq j$.

The assumption stated in Equation 5.15, that the variances of the person-specific error-score random variables for person p are *not* necessarily equal when the tests are tau-equivalent, differs from the equality hypothesis stated for parallel tests in Equation 5.2. Several consequences follow from the possibility of unequal person-specific error variances.

(1) The hypothesis of tau-equivalence does *not* imply, as does the hypothesis of parallelism, that the observed-score variances, $\sigma^2_{X_1}$ and $\sigma^2_{X_2}$, of the tests should be equal. (To see this, consider again Equation 3.4—$\sigma^2_X = \sigma^2_T + \sigma^2_E$—which applies to both random variables X_1 and X_2. Because of the equal true-score hypothesis stated in Equation 5.14, the variances of the true-score random variables of two tau-equivalent tests, $\sigma^2_{T_1}$ and $\sigma^2_{T_2}$, must be equal. But the assumption stated in Equation 5.15

means that the expected-values of the person-specific error variances for the two tests, $\varepsilon_p[\sigma^2_{E_{1p}}]$ and $\varepsilon_p[\sigma^2_{E_{2p}}]$, are not necessarily equal. This means it is not necessary, for tau-equivalent tests, that the error variance $\sigma^2_{E_1}$ should equal the error variance $\sigma^2_{E_2}$. Combining these results, we see it is no longer necessary that $\sigma^2_{X_1} = \sigma^2_{T_1} + \sigma^2_{E_1}$ should equal $\sigma^2_{T_2} + \sigma^2_{E_2} = \sigma^2_{X_2}$.)

(2) Coefficients of correlation involving different tau-equivalent instruments need not necessarily be equal, as must be the case for parallel tests. Symbolically, this means, for observed-score random variables X_i, X_j, and X_k for tau-equivalent tests $i, j, k, \ldots$, and for observed-score random variable Y for the measure of another characteristic, that $\rho_{X_iX_j} \neq \rho_{X_iX_k} \neq \ldots$ and $\rho_{X_iY} \neq \rho_{X_jY} \neq \ldots$. This follows because the coefficient of correlation between a tau-equivalent measure and either another tau-equivalent measure or the measure of another variable altogether involves the standard deviations of the variables, as well as their covariance; although the covariance coefficients for tau-equivalent tests will be identical, the differing standard deviations make the correlation coefficients unequal.

(3) The coefficients of reliability for tau-equivalent tests can differ from one test to another. Although each member of a set of tau-equivalent measures must have equal true-score variances, as has already been noted, the fact that observed-score variances can differ means that the coefficient of reliability (defined as the ratio of true-score variance to observed-score variance) need not be the same for each tau-equivalent measure.

The numerical expectations we can entertain for the observed-score random variables of tau-equivalent tests are illustrated in Table 5.2.

The Hypothesis of Essentially Tau-Equivalent Tests

The assumptions defining the hypothesis of essential tau-equivalence for two tests are that

$$(1) \quad \tau_{1p} = \tau_{2p} + c_{12}, \tag{5.16}$$

and also that

$$(2) \quad \sigma^2_{E_{1p}} \neq \sigma^2_{E_{2p}}, \tag{5.17}$$

TABLE 5.2 Numerical Illustration of Equivalent and Nonequivalent Statistics for Three Tau-Equivalent Tests and Another Variable

Variable Designation	Expected Values (μ)	Vari- ances* σ^2	Relia- bility** Coefficients	Coefficients of Covariance / Correlation†			
				X_1	X_2	X_3	Y
Tau-Eq. Test 1 (X_1)	100	225	0.92	—	207	207	78
Tau-Eq. Test 2 (X_2)	100	256	0.81	0.86	—	207	78
Tau-Eq. Test 3 (X_3)	100	289	0.72	0.81	0.76	—	78
Another Variable (Y)	70	64	0.80	0.65	0.61	0.57	—

* The variances of the observed-score random variables were obtained on the assumption that $\sigma_{T_i}^2 = 207$ ($i = 1, 2, 3$) and that $\sigma_{E_1}^2 = 18$, $\sigma_{E_2}^2 = 49$, and $\sigma_{E_3}^2 = 82$.
** The coefficient of reliability for each tau-equivalent test was obtained by dividing the variance of the true-score random variable for each test (equal to 207) by the variance of the observed-score random variable for the test, and rounding the result to two decimal places.
† Coefficients of covariance are above the diagonal, which is marked by dashes (—), and coefficients of correlation are below the diagonal. The coefficients of correlation, which were rounded to two decimal places, vary inversely with the magnitude of the standard deviations of the tau-equivalent tests. These standard deviations are 15, 16, and 17 for X_1, X_2, and X_3, respectively.

with new term c_{12} of Equation 5.16 a constant linking the true-scores, for person p, on two essentially tau-equivalent tests. This constant is the same, according to Equation 5.16, for all persons p.

The hypothesis of essential tau-equivalence implies only one important difference in expected statistical results from those anticipated for tau-equivalent tests. The additive constant c_{12} linking the true scores on two essentially tau-equivalent tests means that the expected values of the observed-score random variables for the two tests can differ, with the magnitude of the difference being equal to the constant c_{12}. [That is, $\varepsilon(X_1) - \varepsilon(X_2) = \mu_{X_1} - \mu_{X_2} = c_{12}$.] In other words, the constant c_{12} means that the tests can be unequal in difficulty, such that scores on one test tend to be larger than scores on the other test. The expectations for all the other statistics for tau-equivalent tests—variances, coefficients of covariance, coefficients of correlation, and coefficients of reliability— are the same as they were for tau-equivalent tests. This fact is illustrated numerically in Table 5.3.

The Congeneric Test Hypothesis

The final alternative to the hypothesis of parallelism that we consider here is that the tests are linked in a congeneric relationship. The basic assumptions underlying this hypothesis are as follows:

TABLE 5.3 Numerical Illustration of Equivalent and Nonequivalent Statistics for Three Essentially Tau-Equivalent Tests* and Another Variable

Variable Designation	Expected Values (μ)	Vari- ances σ^2	Relia- bility** Coefficients	Coefficients of Covariance / Correlation†			
				X_1	X_2	X_3	Y
Ess. Tau-Eq. Test 1 (X_1)	100	225	0.92	—	207	207	78
Ess. Tau-Eq. Test 2 (X_2)	95	256	0.81	0.86	—	207	78
Ess. Tau-Eq. Test 3 (X_3)	105	289	0.72	0.81	0.76	—	78
Another Variable (Y)	70	64	0.80	0.65	0.61	0.57	—

* The additive constants relating the true scores of the three essentially tau-equivalent tests, X_1, X_2, and X_3, are as follows: $c_{12} = 5$; $c_{13} = -5$; and $c_{23} = -10$; where c_{ij} is the additive constant in the equation $\tau_{ip} = \tau_{jp} + c_{ij}$, where i, j can assume values 1, 2, and 3, respectively.
** The coefficient of reliability for each tau-equivalent test was obtained by dividing the variance of the true-score random variable for each test (equal to 207) by the variance of the observed-score random variable for the test, and rounding the result to two decimal places.
† Coefficients of covariance are above the diagonal, which is marked by dashes (—), and coefficients of correlation are below the diagonal. The coefficients of correlation, which were rounded to two decimal places, vary inversely with the magnitude of the standard deviations of the tau-equivalent tests. These standard deviations are 15, 16, and 17 for X_1, X_2, and X_3, respectively.

$$(1) \quad \tau_{1p} = a_{12}\tau_{2p} + b_{12}, \tag{5.18}$$

and, as for tau-equivalence and essential tau-equivalence,

$$(2) \quad \sigma^2_{E_{1p}} \neq \sigma^2_{E_{2p}}. \tag{5.19}$$

The new terms in Equation 5.18 are a_{12}, the multiplicative constant of the linear transformation required to go from the scale of true scores on Test 2 to the scale of true scores on Test 1, and b_{12}, the additive constant of this transformation.

The additive constant b_{12} of Equation 5.18 causes the expected values of the observed-score random variables for the two tests to differ in the same way that the additive constant c_{12} of Equation 5.16 caused the expected values of the observed-score random variables for two essentially tau-equivalent tests to differ. In addition, however, the multiplicative constant a_{12} has the effect of rescaling the difference in the expected values of observed-score random variables X_1 and X_2, such that this difference depends on a_{12} and on the size of the expected value of the observed score variable for one or the other test. This is shown in the following equation:

$$\varepsilon(X_2) - \varepsilon(X_1) = \mu_{X_2} - \mu_{X_1} = (1 - a_{12})\mu_{X_2} - b_{12}. \qquad (5.20)$$

The congeneric hypothesis implies three additional important results: (1) The coefficient of covariance for any pair of tests in a set of three or more congeneric tests can now differ from the coefficient of covariance for any other pair of tests in the set. (2) The covariance coefficient for a pair of variables that includes one member of a set of congeneric tests and the measure of any other characteristic can differ from the corresponding covariance coefficient for any other congeneric measure in the set. (3) The reliability coefficients of congeneric tests can differ. These results are demonstrated in Sidebar 5.2.

The foregoing consequences of the congeneric hypothesis are illustrated numerically in Table 5.4.

Comparing Hypotheses

Several tests designed to measure the same characteristic may not prove to be closely parallel. They may prove, instead, to be more nearly tau-equivalent or essentially tau-equivalent or congeneric. One strategy for deciding which, if any, of these hypotheses is appropriate for a set of tests is to begin with the least restrictive hypothesis, that the tests are congeneric. The degree to which the statistics for a set of tests are satisfied by this hypothesis can then be compared with the degree to which the statistics are satisfied by a more restrictive hypothesis, for example, the hypothesis of essential tau-equivalence. Such a comparison as this is possible provided the more restrictive hypothesis is *nested* in the less restrictive one. Nesting means that the two hypotheses are similar except for a restriction that is imposed on the less restrictive hypothesis, to yield the more restrictive one. The hypothesis of essential tau-equivalence is nested within the hypothesis of congeneric tests because we need only impose a restriction on the multiplicative term (a_{ij}) of the linear transformation relating the true scores of a pair of congeneric tests—that $a_{ij} = 1$ for all $i, j = 1, 2, 3, \ldots$, with $i \neq j$—to obtain the hypothesis of essential tau-equivalence. If the more restrictive hypothesis accounts for the test statistics about as well as the less restrictive hypothesis—a more restrictive hypothesis can never provide a better description than a less restrictive hypothesis, and might produce a markedly worse description—and if the explanation provided by both the more restrictive and the less restrictive hypotheses are good enough (in an overall sense not discussed here; see, e.g., Jöreskog &

Sidebar 5.2

PROOFS OF SEVERAL RESULTS FOR CONGENERIC TESTS

The basic assumption of congeneric tests, stated in Equation 5.18, is restated here for tests i and j ($i, j = 1, 2, 3, \ldots$):

$$\tau_{ip} = a_{ij}\tau_{jp} + b_{ij}. \tag{5.2.1}$$

The assumption presented in Equation 5.19 can also be restated as follows:

$$\sigma^2_{E_{ip}} \neq \sigma^2_{E_{jp}}. \tag{5.2.2}$$

Now consider the covariance between observed-score random variables X_i and X_j. As before

$$\sigma_{X_iX_j} = \sigma_{T_iT_j} \tag{5.2.3}$$

because the error random variables E_i and E_j are assumed to be uncorrelated with themselves and with the true-score random variables T_i and T_j, respectively. Now, because of the relationship expressed in Equation 5.2.1, we have that

$$\sigma_{X_iX_j} = \sigma_{(a_{ij}T_j + b_{ij})T_j} = a_{ij}\sigma^2_{T_j}. \tag{5.2.4}$$

This implies that

$$\sigma_{X_iX_j} \neq \sigma_{X_kX_j}, \tag{5.2.5}$$

provided that $a_{ij} \neq a_{kj}$, for all tests $i, j, k = 1, 2, 3, \ldots$, with $i \neq j \neq k$. This is the first point to be demonstrated here.

As a further point, note that inasmuch as the covariances between different pairs of congeneric tests are not equal, as indicated in Equation 5.2.5, and inasmuch as the standard deviations of congeneric tests are not equal—the assumption stated in Equation 5.1.1 implies $\sigma^2_{T_i} \neq \sigma^2_{T_j}$ and the assumption stated in Equation 5.1.2 implies $\sigma^2_{E_i} \neq \sigma^2_{E_j}$, and together these imply that

$$\sigma^2_{X_i} = \sigma^2_{T_i} + \sigma^2_{E_i} \neq \sigma^2_{T_j} + \sigma^2_{E_j} = \sigma^2_{X_j}, \tag{5.2.6}$$

—it follows that

Sörbom, 1989), then one might be justified in concluding that the more restrictive hypothesis is acceptable for the tests. In general, more restrictive hypotheses are preferred to less restrictive hypothesis. The former provides a simpler description of the relationships among a set of tests, simpler in the sense that fewer different parameters are required

---

Sidebar 5.2 Continued

$$\rho_{X_i X_j} = \frac{\sigma_{X_i X_j}}{\sigma_{X_i}\sigma_{X_j}} \neq \rho_{X_k X_j} = \frac{\sigma_{X_k X_j}}{\sigma_{X_k}\sigma_{X_j}}, \tag{5.2.7}$$

again for all tests $i, j, k = 1, 2, 3, \ldots$, with $i \neq j \neq k$.

In a similar fashion, it can be shown that

$$\sigma_{X_i Y} = a_{ij}\sigma_{T_j Y} \neq \sigma_{T_j Y} = \sigma_{X_j Y}, \tag{5.2.8}$$

except when $a_{ij} = 1$. (The latter condition on a_{ij} would imply the hypothesis of essential tau-equivalence instead of the hypothesis of congeneric tests.) This is the second point that was to be demonstrated here. And because of the result given in Equation 5.2.8, together with the fact that $\sigma_{X_i} \neq \sigma_{X_j}$, as shown in Equation 5.2.6, it is also the case that

$$\rho_{X_i Y} \neq \rho_{X_j Y}. \tag{5.2.9}$$

A final result is that the reliabilities of congeneric tests are not equal. From Equation 5.2.1,

$$\sigma_{T_i}^2 = a_{ij}^2\sigma_{T_j}^2, \tag{5.2.10}$$

so, in general, given $a_{ij} \neq 1$,

$$\sigma_{T_i}^2 \neq \sigma_{T_j}^2. \tag{5.2.11}$$

Putting the result in Equation 5.2.11 together with that in Equation 5.2.6, we have that

$$\rho_{X_i}^2 = \frac{\sigma_{T_i}^2}{\sigma_{X_i}^2} \neq \rho_{X_j}^2 = \frac{\sigma_{T_j}^2}{\sigma_{X_j}^2}. \tag{5.2.12}$$

These results are illustrated numerically in Table 5.4.

---

in the description. Otherwise, the tentative conclusion could be drawn that the less restrictive hypothesis is to be preferred. If the more restrictive hypothesis is the winner, it can be put in competition with an even more restrictive hypothesis, provided that hypothesis is nested within the less restrictive one. (The hypothesis of tau-equivalence is

TABLE 5.4 Numerical Illustration of Equivalent and Nonequivalent Statistics for Three Congeneric Tests* and Another Variable

Variable Designation	Expected Values (μ)	Vari- ances σ^2	Reli- ability** Coefficients	Coefficients of Covariance / Correlation†			
				X_1	X_2	X_3	Y
Congeneric Test 1 (X_1)	100.00	225.00	0.92	—	172.50	230.00	78.00
Congeneric Test 2 (X_2)	79.17	192.75	0.75	0.83	—	191.67	65.00
Congeneric Test 3 (X_3)	116.67	336.56	0.76	0.84	0.75	—	86.67
Another Variable (Y)	70.00	64.00	0.80	0.65	0.59	0.59	—

* The linear transformations relating the true scores of the three congeneric tests, X_1, X_2, and X_3, are as follows: $\tau_{1p} = 1.2\tau_{2p} + 5$; $\tau_{1p} = 0.9\tau_{3p} - 5$; $\tau_{2p} = 0.75\tau_{3p} - 8.33$.
** The coefficient of reliability for each congeneric test was obtained by dividing the variance of the true-score random variable for each test by the variance of the observed-score random variable for the test, and rounding the result to two decimal places. The variances of the true-score random variables were derived using the transformations given in the above note of this table, assuming that $\sigma_{T_1}^2 = 207$. The variances of the observed-score random variables were derived on the basis of the further assumptions that $\sigma_{E_1}^2 = 18$, $\sigma_{E_2}^2 = 49$, and $\sigma_{E_3}^2 = 82$.
† Coefficients of covariance are above the diagonal, which is marked by dashes (—), and coefficients of correlation are below the diagonal. The coefficients of covariance among congeneric variables X_1, X_2, and X_3 are equal to the coefficients of covariance among the corresponding true-score variables T_1, T_2, and T_3. The latter covariance coefficients can be derived noting the transformations in the first note and the assumption that $\sigma_{T_1}^2 = 207$.

nested within that of essential tau-equivalence, and the hypothesis of parallel tests is nested within that of tau-equivalence.) If it can be demonstrated at some point that one hypothesis is to be preferred above all others and that this hypothesis provides a reasonable account of the statistics available for the tests, then it can be used as a basis for estimating reliability coefficients and standard errors of measurement.

Whenever we cannot accept the parallel or tau-equivalent or essentially tau-equivalent or congeneric hypothesis for a set of tests, we must resort to an even less restrictive test theory than that of congeneric tests. One such theory is known as generalizability theory, the topic of the book by Shavelson and Webb (1991) in this series.

Summary

The concept of parallel tests has been defined, and it has been shown that if it is possible to construct parallel or very nearly parallel tests,

TABLE 5.5 Some Models for Reliability Theory

Hypothesis	Assumptions*	Equivalencies	Implications / Interpretations
1. Parallel Tests (designated 1, 2, 3, ...)	$\tau_{1p} = \tau_{2p} = \tau_{3p} = \ldots$	$\mu_{X_1} = \mu_{X_2} = \mu_{X_3} = \ldots$	Equal expected values of observed-score random variables.
	$\sigma^2_{E_{1p}} = \sigma^2_{E_{2p}} = \sigma^2_{E_{3p}} = \ldots$	$\sigma_{X_1} = \sigma_{X_2} = \sigma_{X_3} = \ldots$	Equal standard deviations of observed-score random variables.
		$\sigma_{X_1X_2} = \sigma_{X_1X_3} = \sigma_{X_2X_3} = \ldots$ $\sigma_{X_1Y} = \sigma_{X_2Y} = \sigma_{X_3Y} = \ldots$	Equal covariances of observed-score random variables for any pair of parallel tests, or for any pair consisting of one of the parallel tests and a test of another characteristic.
		$\rho_{X_1X_2} = \rho_{X_1X_3} = \rho_{X_2X_3} = \ldots$ $\rho_{X_1Y} = \rho_{X_2Y} = \rho_{X_3Y} = \ldots$	Equal coefficients of correlation, corresponding to the equal covariances.
		$\rho^2_{X_1} = \rho^2_{X_2} = \rho^2_{X_3} = \ldots$	Equal coefficients of reliability.
2. Tau-Equivalent Tests (designated 1, 2, 3, ...)	$\tau_{1p} = \tau_{2p} = \tau_{3p} = \ldots$	$\mu_{X_1} = \mu_{X_2} = \mu_{X_3} = \ldots$	Equal expected values of observed-score random variables.
	$\sigma^2_{E_{1p}} \neq \sigma^2_{E_{2p}} \neq \sigma^2_{E_{3p}} \neq \ldots$	$\sigma_{X_1} \neq \sigma_{X_2} \neq \sigma_{X_3} \neq \ldots$	Standard deviations differ.
		$\sigma_{X_1X_2} = \sigma_{X_1X_3} = \sigma_{X_2X_3} = \ldots$	Equal covariances, as for parallel tests.
		$\sigma_{X_1Y} = \sigma_{X_2Y} = \sigma_{X_3Y} = \ldots$	
		$\rho_{X_1X_2} \neq \rho_{X_1X_3} \neq \rho_{X_2X_3} \neq \ldots$	Coefficients of correlation differ.
		$\rho_{X_1Y} \neq \rho_{X_2Y} \neq \rho_{X_3Y} \neq \ldots$	
		$\rho^2_{X_1} \neq \rho^2_{X_2} \neq \rho^2_{X_3} \neq \ldots$	Coefficients of reliability differ.

continued

then the means exist to estimate the coefficient of reliability, ρ^2_X, and the standard error of measurement, σ_E of the tests. In addition, several alternatives to the parallel test hypothesis were considered, alternatives

TABLE 5.5 Continued

Hypothesis	Assumptions*	Equivalencies	Implications / Interpretations
3. Essentially Tau-Equivalent Tests (designated $i, j, k, \ldots$)	$\tau_{ip} = \tau_{jp} + c_{ij}$**	$\mu_{X_1} \neq \mu_{X_2} \neq \mu_{X_3} \neq \ldots$	Expected values of observed-score random variables differ.
	$\sigma_{E_{1p}}^2 \neq \sigma_{E_{2p}}^2 \neq \sigma_{E_{3p}}^2 \neq \ldots$	$\sigma_{X_1} \neq \sigma_{X_2} \neq \sigma_{X_3} \neq \ldots$	Standard deviations differ.
		$\sigma_{X_i X_j} = \sigma_{X_i X_k} = \sigma_{X_j X_k} = \ldots$	Equal covariances, as for parallel tests.
		$\sigma_{X_i Y} = \sigma_{X_j Y} = \sigma_{X_k Y} = \ldots$	
		$\rho_{X_1 X_2} \neq \rho_{X_1 X_3} \neq \rho_{X_2 X_3} \neq \ldots$	Coefficients of correlation differ.
		$\rho_{X_1 Y} \neq \rho_{X_2 Y} \neq \rho_{X_3 Y} \neq \ldots$	
		$\rho_{X_1}^2 \neq \rho_{X_2}^2 \neq \rho_{X_3}^2 \neq \ldots$	Coefficients of reliability differ.
4. Congeneric Tests (designated $i, j, \ldots$)	$\tau_{ip} = a_{ij}\tau_{jp} + b_{ij}$†	$\mu_{X_1} \neq \mu_{X_2} \neq \mu_{X_3} \neq \ldots$	Expected values of observed-score random variables differ.
	$\sigma_{E_{1p}}^2 \neq \sigma_{E_{2p}}^2 \neq \sigma_{E_{3p}}^2 \neq \ldots$	$\sigma_{X_1} \neq \sigma_{X_2} \neq \sigma_{X_3} \neq \ldots$	Standard deviations differ.
		$\sigma_{X_1 X_2} \neq \sigma_{X_1 X_3} \neq \sigma_{X_2 X_3} \neq \ldots$	Covariances differ.
		$\sigma_{X_1 Y} \neq \sigma_{X_2 Y} \neq \sigma_{X_3 Y} \neq \ldots$	
		$\rho_{X_1 X_2} \neq \rho_{X_1 X_3} \neq \rho_{X_2 X_3} \neq \ldots$	Coefficients of correlation differ.
		$\rho_{X_1 Y} \neq \rho_{X_2 Y} \neq \rho_{X_3 Y} \neq \ldots$	
		$\rho_{X_1}^2 \neq \rho_{X_2}^2 \neq \rho_{X_3}^2 \neq \ldots$	Coefficients of reliability differ.

* In addition, the basic assumptions and results of reliability theory, as presented in Chapter 3, are assumed for all hypotheses.
** c_{ij} is a constant linking the expected-value true scores of essentially tau-equivalent tests i and j, this constant being the same for all persons p.
† a_{ij} and b_{ij} are, respectively, the slope and intercept of the linear transformation linking the expected-value true scores of congeneric tests i and j, the transformation being the same for all persons p.

that impose somewhat less restrictive conditions on various statistics for a set of tests than the conditions imposed by the hypothesis of parallel tests. The hypotheses that were considered, and the implications of each for the expected values, variances, covariance coefficients, correlation coefficients, and reliability coefficients of the observed-score random variables of a set of tests are summarized in Table 5.5.

Exercises

5.1. For a certain population of examinees, the standard deviation of the observed-score random variable for a test is 15 and the expected value is 100. What are the expected value and standard deviation of the observed-score random variable for a parallel test?

5.2. Given that $\sigma_X^2 = 400$ and $\rho_X^2 = 0.92$, calculate the value of σ_E^2.

5.3. Assume four tests are "congeneric" according to the definition given in Chapter 5. Insofar as it is possible to do so, complete the following table of information about these tests by writing the appropriate numbers in the blanks:

Test	1	2	3	4	μ_X	σ_X
1	1.00	—[1]	54	60	55	7
2	0.75	1.00	63	70	53	8
3	0.77	—[2]	1.00	90	54	—[3]
4	0.78	0.80	0.82	1.00	—[4]	11

NOTE: The following comment does not apply to the columns headed μ_X and σ_X. The covariance between the pair of variables identified by a given combination of row number and column number appears in the cell for which the identifying row number is smaller than the identifying column number. These cells lie above and to the right of the cells of the main diagonal (upper left to lower right). Coefficients of correlation appear both in the diagonal cells and in the cells below the diagonal. These are the cells for which the identifying column number is either equal to or smaller than the identifying row number.

Note

1. Here and in subsequent chapters, the numbers 1, 2, 3, and the like, or the letters i, j, k, and the like, are often used as subscripts to designate particular tests or particular random variables. When it is necessary, in order for the reference to a test or random variable to be clear, the letter designating the test or variable will also be present as a subscript, as in μ_{X_1} or σ_{X_j}, otherwise only the numerical or letter subscript will appear, as in σ_j^2 (meaning $\sigma_{X_j}^2$).

6

Experiments and Formulas for Estimating a
Reliability Coefficient

Estimating a reliability coefficient for a measuring procedure involves conducting an experiment. In this chapter, we consider some of the basic conditions that reliability experiments should satisfy. Then we describe several different approaches to the conduct of reliability experiments and identify the sources of variation to which each is sensitive. For each approach we also describe one or more ways of calculating estimates of a reliability coefficient from the data collected in the experiment.

Before tackling the agenda outlined in the foregoing paragraph, we note the fact that reliability coefficients are almost always calculated from the measurements taken of samples of persons, not whole populations. Thus the usual reliability experiment provides a sample *estimate* of the reliability coefficient for the population. Had a different sample of persons participated in the experiment, the reliability coefficient obtained would almost certainly have been a different number. In recognition of this fact, we refer to reliability coefficients computed from measurements for samples of examinees as *estimates* of population reliability coefficients. The ^ symbol is used to differentiate sample estimates from population parameters throughout this book. Consequently, whenever an *estimate* of a reliability coefficient is produced, it is denoted as such by adding the ^ symbol to the symbol for the reliability coefficient; that is, $\hat{\rho}_X^2$ refers to an estimate of the reliability coefficient calculated from the measurements taken of a sample of examinees.

Factors to Consider in Conducting Reliability Experiments

The acts of recruiting examinees for a reliability experiment and administering the measurement procedures should satisfy at least four conditions. The sample should be representative of the population of examinees that is of interest, the measurements should be experimentally independent, the procedure for collecting data in the reliability experiment should duplicate that used in practical applications of the measuring instrument, and the experiment should produce at least two measurements on every participant. These conditions are discussed further in the following paragraphs. But first we consider the factor of sample size.

Sample Size. Other factors being held constant, the larger the sample, the more precise we expect the estimate of reliability to be. Although the exact mathematical form of the sampling distribution for a particular estimate of a reliability coefficient is not usually known, in general we expect the standard error of the estimate of a statistical parameter to be inversely related to the square root of the sample size. (The sampling distribution for an estimate of a parameter describes the extent to which the estimate can be expected to vary from one randomly equivalent sample to another. The standard error referred to is the standard deviation of the sampling distribution of the estimate.) If we wish to halve the standard error of an estimate of reliability, we need to quadruple the sample size. This fact should be borne in mind by anyone who plans to conduct a reliability experiment.

Sample Representativeness. The examinees should be chosen in a way such that they represent a well-defined population. This canon of research is frequently disregarded by researchers in the social sciences. Reliability experiments are often conducted on convenience samples, consisting of persons who are readily available to the experimenter. This approach to sampling is not satisfactory for tests advertised as having been standardized on a particular population of examinees. Low cost may justify the use of "grab-bag" samples in relatively small-scale research studies. It is important to realize, however, that the extent to which reliability coefficients based on grab-bag samples can be generalized beyond the sample itself will be uncertain; the reason lies in the impossibility of describing the population from which the sample was drawn, let alone describing the relationship of the sample to the population.

Experimental Independence of the Measurements. By experimental independence of the measurements we mean, in part, that the measurement for one examinee must neither have been influenced by nor have influenced the measurement for any other examinee. When the measuring procedure consists of a test administered to a group, the condition of experimental independence means that no examinee should be able to copy the answers of another examinee or otherwise use another examinee's performance as a guide to his or her own performance. Because reliability experiments must yield at least two measurements per examinee—this point is elaborated later in this chapter—the independence requirement extends even further: Each measurement of an examinee should be experimentally independent of every other measurement of the same examinee; when the measurements consist of test scores, the responses used to generate one score should be independent of the responses used to generate another score. So when the reliability experiment involves the repeated administration of a test, the examinee should not know—should neither be told nor be able to read—the responses he or she gave during the previous administration of the test. This aspect of experimental independence carries an even stronger implication when scores on the parts of a test—individual items or sections of the test—are used explicitly in calculating an estimate of reliability: The response an examinee makes to one test part (item or section) should be independent of the responses he or she makes to other test parts.

The requirement of experimental independence is often ignored in practice. It is obviously ignored whenever the reliability experiment involves the administration of a single test, with (as will be shown subsequently) reliability being estimated from examinee responses to individual questions on the test and with the answer to one question on the test being dependent on the answer to a previous question. Another example is provided by typical tests of reading comprehension, in which several questions are based on the same reading passage. (On the other hand, if the measurement units for estimating reliability consist of whole reading passages plus associated test questions, and the score an examinee receives for each measurement unit—reading passage—is the sum of his or her scores on all the items associated with the reading passage, then lack of experimental independence among the questions for a reading passage ceases to be a source of concern.) Experiments in which the same test is administered more than once probably also violate this condition, depending on how easy it is to recall the responses given in a previous administration.

Readers can imagine conducting the following thought experiment to investigate the issue of dependence empirically. Suppose there are n parts, for example, items, to a test, with n even, and these parts are divided into $n/2$ distinct pairs, with the parts in each pair assigned at random to the first and second positions of the pair. Then, for the condition of experimental independence to hold, it should be true for every examinee that the coefficient of correlation between scores on the first and second parts of pairs, this correlation being taken over pairs, will not differ significantly from zero. If the correlation coefficient did differ significantly from zero, then the independence assumption would appear to have been violated.

A consequence of violating the condition of experimental independence is that errors of measurement among the multiple measurements made of the examinees will probably be correlated. It will be recalled that the assumption of uncorrelated errors of measurement on parallel test forms was needed in Chapter 5 in demonstrating that the correlation between scores on the multiple measures is an estimate of the reliability coefficient. The extent to which an estimate of reliability will be affected by breaching the condition of experimental independence is usually impossible to ascertain. Suffice it to say, the best reliability experiments involve measuring procedures that do not violate the independence condition in the ways just described.

Identical Administrative Procedures for Both the Experiment and Subsequent Applications. The circumstances that pertain during the experiment must be identical to the circumstances examinees will experience when the measuring procedure is administered in practice. For example, the coefficient of reliability that would apply to the condition of 30 minutes of testing time might not pertain to the condition of 40 minutes of testing time. With 40 minutes of testing time, almost all examinees might have time to finish the test without resorting to such strategies as guessing and pattern-marking[1] answers, whereas with only 30 minutes of testing time most examinees might not be able to complete the test unless they guess or pattern-mark answers to the final few items. Different kinds and relative proportions of error variance in total test variance may be expected under the two time limits. Other factors, such as the physical surroundings (lighting, noise level of the testing environment) and the physical and mental condition of the persons being measured, should also be the same for both the reliability experiment and the practical application of the procedure.

Two or More Measurements. A reliability experiment must yield more than one score or measurement for each participant. At least two scores are needed for each person in order to estimate reliability by one of the methods to be discussed. The required scores can be generated, for example, through experiments in which a measuring procedure is employed more than once. For instance, the same instrument (test) could be administered twice, perhaps on different occasions. The probability of violating the independence assumption in this case will be relatively high, and as was indicated earlier, the effect of this violation on the reliability coefficient is usually unknown. More desirable, for the reason that violations of the independence assumption are less likely, is repeated testing that involves the use of parallel or tau-equivalent or essentially tau-equivalent or congeneric forms of tests. Frequently, however, multiple measurements will be obtained for each person from the administration of just one test only once. It is possible, for example, to derive more than one score for a person on a test composed of a number of items or parts, for then the items or parts can themselves be regarded as duplicate measuring instruments. These different approaches to conducting the reliability experiment are considered in the following sections of this chapter. The reader is reminded again that although these discussions are cast in terms of tests, the concepts can be adapted for any measuring procedure used in social science research.

Estimating Reliability by Testing More Than Once

As has been noted, one type of reliability experiment involves testing examinees more than once, each time with a complete instrument. Either the same test is administered on each occasion, or a different test is used each time. If the same instrument is used, the resulting reliability estimate is referred to as a *test-retest coefficient of reliability*. If different instruments are administered each time, the resulting coefficient is referred to as an *alternate-forms estimate of reliability*.

Regardless of which type of coefficient is computed—each is dealt with in greater detail shortly—an important factor to bear in mind in interpreting the coefficient is the length of time between testing occasions. The length of the inter-test interval may be associated with the size of the resulting reliability coefficient, at least for many pencil-and-paper measures of cognitive ability, scholastic achievement, personality, and attitude. We expect the coefficient of reliability to be larger when the time between measurements is relatively short than when the time interval is relatively long—the shortest possible inter-test interval would be that for experiments in which the second testing began immediately after the first had been completed. Examinees are very likely to recall more questions and answers from the previous administration when the interval is short than when it is long. Also, examinees can be expected to change less during a short than a long inter-test interval, in the myriad other ways that might influence test performance. Because these changes are greater for some examinees than others, whatever the length of the inter-test interval, and because the changes will be different in kind for different examinees, they—the changes—tend to make the scores obtained on the first occasion unpredictably different from the scores obtained on a subsequent occasion. It follows that when a repeated-testing experiment is conducted to estimate a reliability coefficient, the length of the interval between testing occasions should be reported together with the estimate of the reliability coefficient that is obtained.

Source of Extraneous Variance in Standard Errors of Measurement Estimated From Data Collected in Test-Retest Reliability Experiments

Reliability experiments are not only conducted for the purpose of estimating a reliability coefficient. These experiments also help us find out something about the magnitude of measurement errors. Ideally, a reliability experiment would enable us to estimate σ_{E_p}, the specific standard error of measurement for person p. Failing this, we would be able to estimate σ_E, the expected value of σ_{E_p} over persons. Estimates of exactly these quantities can be obtained whenever there exist two or more parallel tests; that is, whenever we have tests that produce measurements known to satisfy exactly the hypothesis of parallel tests. But we are very unlikely to have parallel tests—even if we had them, we could never be sure—so the estimates of the standard error of measurement we obtain will be inflated by the departures from parallelism that are associated with the reliability experiment being conducted. Each different design for reliability experiments is sensitive to different kinds of departures from parallelism in the replicate measurements obtained in the experiment. We consider in this section at least some of the reasons why departures from parallelism can be expected to arise in the conduct of test-retest reliability experiments.

A person's standing on the characteristic being measured in a test-retest experiment can fluctuate from one testing to the next, with the fluctuation for one person very likely to differ in direction and extent from the fluctuation for another person. One source of fluctuations in test scores is the learning—more generally, the real change in status on the variable being measured—that occurs between testing occasions. This learning or real change, which may be prompted, at least in part, by the initial testing, is very likely to vary from examinee to examinee due to the content being examined. Some examinees, for example, will find it easier to learn a particular body of content (e.g., biology) than will other examinees. Another source of change in test scores may be ability to recall questions (and answers) from the first administration of the test to the next, with this ability being possessed to a greater extent by some examinees than by others. Score changes also may be due to the physical states of the examinees, which will not be constant over time. In addition, the conditions of testing will not be exactly the same from one occasion to the next. All these sources of variation in test scores will add to the estimate of the standard error of measurement based on data collected in a test-retest experiment, at least to the extent that their effects on test scores are differential. Examinee changes in scores from one testing occasion to another are differential when they are not constant for all examinees, but vary from examinee to examinee in a way that is both unpredictable and results in a different ordering of examinees from occasion to occasion. Statisticians refer to this as variation in test scores due to examinee-by-occasion interaction.

The magnitude of the effect of examinee-by-occasion interaction on test scores is very likely to be greater the longer the time interval between the testing occasions. But this interaction effect is possible, even when the multiple administrations of a test occur one right after the other. For example, if the test is long, fatigue would be expected to interact with performances on a test repeated in a short period of time. This person-by-occasion interaction will increase the estimate of the standard error of measurement beyond what the standard error would be were there no such interaction.

Is it a bad thing that estimates of the standard error of measurement will be inflated by the person-by-occasion interaction present in the data collected in a test-retest reliability experiment? Yes, it is, in that what we would like to know is σ_{E_p} or σ_E, and estimates of these quantities will be inflated by the presence of person-by-occasion interaction. In the reality of the test-retest experiment, however, it is impossible to produce estimates of σ_{E_p} or σ_E free of this interaction. We need to be aware of this fact in interpreting the estimates of σ_{E_p} or σ_E that are produced from data collected in a test-retest experiment.

Sources of Extraneous Variance in Standard Errors of Measurement Estimated From Data Collected in Reliability Experiments in Which Alternate Forms of a Test Are Administered on Different Occasions

Extraneous contributions to estimates of the standard error of measurement similar to the extraneous contributions described in the preceding section may be expected for the reliability experiment in which a different instrument is administered on each of two or more testing occasions. During the interval of time between the testing occasions of this experiment, we may expect test scores to be affected by person-by-occasion interactions of the sort noted for the test-retest experiment. In addition, however, the contents of the tests used in the alternate-forms reliability experiment will differ. This variation in content introduces a new potential source of interaction variance between the content of the different instruments and the examinees being assessed. This component of variance will affect the estimate of the standard error of measurement from an alternate-forms reliability experiment, but this component of variance is not present to affect the estimate of the standard error of measurement from a test-retest experiment

Consider an example of content-by-person interaction: Suppose pronounced differences were known to exist among vocabulary tests in the domains of knowledge represented by the words appearing in them. If one such test had a preponderance of history-related words and another had a preponderance of science-related words, then the first test would tend to favor examinees who had done more reading about history, whereas the second test would tend to favor examinees who had done more reading about science. If the objective of the tests was to assess general knowledge of vocabulary, then variations in test scores due to differences in the domains of words sampled by one test as compared with another, when that variation is unplanned and unsystematic, would add to the estimate of the standard error of measurement derived from the test scores.[2]

We now turn our attention to the matter of calculating an estimate of reliability from the data collected in a repeated-testing experiment.

Calculating Estimates of Reliability

The simplest way to obtain an estimate of reliability in the present context is to calculate the coefficient of correlation between the test scores obtained on the two occasions. When it can be presumed that the test scores satisfy certain conditions, the resulting coefficient of correlation can be interpreted (in the sense of Chapter 5) as an estimate of the reliability coefficient of the test used on either occasion. The conditions that must be satisfied are these: The measurements taken of each person on the two occasions are either (1) parallel (i.e., for occasions 1 and 2 and for each person p, $\tau_{2p} = \tau_{1p}$ and $\sigma_{E_{2p}} = \sigma_{E_{1p}}$, or (2) have linearly related true scores and standard errors of measurement (i.e., again for occasions 1 and 2, $\tau_{2p} = m\tau_{1p} + n$ and $\sigma_{E_{2p}} = m\sigma_{E_{1p}}$, where m and n are, respectively, the slope and intercept of the linear transformation relating τ_{1p} and τ_{2p}, and the same value of m is the slope of the transformation relating $\sigma_{E_{1p}}$ and $\sigma_{E_{2p}}$, for all persons p). This latter condition allows for differences in the means and variances of the distributions of scores for the two occasions. It might be that the distribution for the second occasion has a larger (or smaller) mean and greater (or lesser) variability than the distribution for the first occasion, a result that may be attributed either to a practice effect or, in the event a different test form is used each time, to a difference in the difficulty of the forms or to a difference in their capacity to discriminate among examinees, or to both causes. Theoretical derivations supporting the foregoing assertion are provided in Sidebar 6.1.

Another approach to the estimation of reliability from the scores obtained on two testing occasions is to conduct an analysis of variance of the scores. (The theoretical basis for this approach is not given here—it can be studied in the book by Lord and Novick, 1968, chap. 7.) Under the assumption that the tests on the two occasions are parallel, estimates of the variances of the true-score random variable and the error random variable can be derived from the mean-squares of a one-way analysis of variance (ANOVA), with the examinees themselves defining the independent variable of the ANOVA. The mean-square residual of this analysis, say MS_{Res}, is an estimate of σ_E^2, and the difference between the mean square for persons, say MS_p, and that for the mean-square residual, divided by the number of measurements taken of each examinee, say n, is the estimate of σ_T^2. The estimate of reliability is then

$$\hat{\rho}_X^2 = \frac{\hat{\sigma}_T^2}{\hat{\sigma}_T^2 + \hat{\sigma}_E^2}$$
$$= \frac{\frac{1}{n}(MS_p - MS_{Res})}{\frac{1}{n}(MS_p - MS_{Res}) + MS_{Res}}$$
$$= \frac{MS_p - MS_{Res}}{MS_p + (n-1)MS_{Res}}$$

A one-way ANOVA is easily performed on a set of data using such statistical computer programs as MINITAB (MINITAB, 1989).

An example of the calculation of a reliability coefficient using the correlation approach is provided in Sidebar 6.2. For comparison purposes, the corresponding estimate using the analysis of variance approach is also provided.

Estimating Reliability by Testing Only Once

Another type of reliability experiment involves assembling a group of examinees and collecting the requisite repeated measurements from the administration of only one test administered only once. This is a viable design provided the test is divisible into distinct (nonoverlapping) parts, each of which may be viewed as a separate measurement. One possibility is that the test is in two parts and so can yield two scores.[3] A test composed of an even number of items can be divided into two equal-sized sets of items, with each set then being scored separately. Alternatively, the test might consist of two independent parts, for example, two essay questions or two mathematics problems; then each essay or problem can yield a separate score. The processing of the two scores for each examinee so as to produce an estimate of reliability could then proceed in a manner similar to that used with the scores on two complete tests. The (two) part scores derived from a test administered just once could be used to calculate a coefficient of correlation, or they could be subjected instead to an analysis of variance. This would not be the end of the matter, however, for the resulting coefficient would pertain to the reliability of either of the two scores considered separately, not to the composite of both scores. We deal with this complication shortly.

Sources of Extraneous Variance in Estimates of the Standard Error of Measurement From Single-Administration Reliability Experiments

The standard error of estimate that is derived from the scores examinees obtain on a test administered on only a single occasion will be affected by extraneous variance (in the sense defined earlier in this chapter) from at least one source—the interaction of examinees with test content. This interaction is possible because content varies from one part of the test to another, just as it does in the alternate-forms reliability experiment. In addition, differential examinee fatigue may be a source of extraneous variance, particularly if the test parts consist of the

---

Sidebar 6.1

A PROOF CONCERNING THE COEFFICIENT OF CORRELATION AS AN
ESTIMATOR OF THE COEFFICIENT OF RELIABILITY

This is a proof that the Pearson product-moment coefficient of correlation between scores on two tests provides an estimate of the reliability of either test when the true scores and the variances of the person-specific variables of the examinees are linearly related.

Assume that the person-specific observed-score random variables X_{1p} and X_{2p} for person p ($p = 1, 2, 3, \ldots$) have true- and error-score components as follows:

$$X_{ip} = \tau_{ip} + E_{ip} \qquad (6.1.1)$$

for test i ($i = 1, 2$). Also assume that the expected value true scores and the variances of the person-specific error random variables of the two tests are linearly related as follows:

$$\tau_{2p} = m\tau_{1p} + n \qquad (6.1.2)$$

and

$$\sigma_{E_{2p}} = m\sigma_{E_{1p}}, \qquad (6.1.3)$$

where $\sigma_{E_{ip}}$ ($i = 1, 2$) is the person-specific standard error of measurement for person p on test i.

It follows from these assumptions and the usual assumptions of classical reliability theory (see Chapters 3 and 5) that

$$\sigma_{X_1 X_2} = \sigma_{T_1 T_2}$$

$$= \sigma_{(T_1, \, mT_1 + n)}$$

$$= m\sigma_{T_1}^2 . \qquad (6.1.4)$$

Also,

$$\sigma_{X_1}^2 = \sigma_{T_1}^2 + \sigma_{E_1}^2$$

$$= \sigma_{T_1}^2 + \varepsilon_p[\sigma_{E_{1p}}^2] \qquad (6.1.5)$$

---

first half of the test versus the second half. If, however, the test is composed of items, and the test parts can be constructed by partitioning the items into the set of odd-numbered items versus the set of even-numbered items, then differential fatigue will affect performance of each part more or less equally and will not be a serious source of extraneous variance.

Sidebar 6.1 Continued

and

$$\sigma^2_{X_2} = \sigma^2_{T_2} + \sigma^2_{E_2}$$

$$= \sigma^2_{T_2} + \varepsilon_p[\sigma^2_{E_{2p}}]$$

$$= m^2\sigma^2_{T_1} + m^2\varepsilon_p[\sigma^2_{E_{1p}}]$$

$$= m^2[\sigma^2_{T_1} + \sigma^2_{E_1}]$$

$$= m^2\sigma^2_{X_1}. \tag{6.1.6}$$

Substituting the results demonstrated in Equations 6.1.4 and 6.1.6 into an expression for the coefficient of correlation between observed-score variables X_1 and X_2 (see, e.g., Equation 5.11), we obtain the following expression:

$$\rho_{X_1 X_2} = \frac{\sigma_{X_1 X_2}}{\sigma_{X_1}\sigma_{X_2}}$$

$$= \frac{m\sigma^2_{T_1}}{(\sigma_{X_1})(m\sigma_{X_1})}$$

$$= \frac{\sigma^2_{T_1}}{\sigma^2_{X_1}},$$

which, by definition, is the reliability of X_1.

By analogous argument, it can be shown that

$$\rho_{X_1 X_2} = \frac{\sigma^2_{T_2}}{\sigma^2_{X_2}},$$

which also, by definition, is the reliability of X_2.

Calculating Estimates of Reliability

As has been noted, estimating the coefficient of reliability from the data provided by a single test administered only once is not straightforward, contrary to what one might expect. Consider the case in which the test yields two scores. In an ideal scenario, these are scores on parallel half-tests, and so the correlation between the scores provides

Sidebar 6.2

A DEMONSTRATION OF THE CALCULATION OF AN ESTIMATE OF
RELIABILITY USING TWO DIFFERENT APPROACHES

The following data consist of the scores of 20 examinees on each of two intelligence tests administered on two occasions, the interval between occasions being 1 week.

Person	Test 1	Test 2
1	83	90
2	122	126
3	84	82
4	87	83
5	70	70
6	107	99
7	105	113
8	119	117
9	110	111
10	110	102
11	113	114
12	80	80
13	102	103
14	88	89
15	117	111
16	119	119
17	105	102
18	96	100
19	96	101
20	87	87

an estimate of the reliability of either *half-test*. What we want, however, is the reliability of scores on the total test. The solution is to *correct* the coefficient of correlation between scores on the half-test using the Spearman-Brown formula to obtain an estimate of what the coefficient would have been had two whole tests been administered. This formula and the theory underlying it are provided in the following section. Also considered are other ways of estimating a reliability coefficient from data obtained in a single-test, single-session experiment.

Sidebar 6.2 Continued

Correlation Estimate of Reliability

	Test 1		Test 2
Mean	100.00		99.95
SD	15.09		14.96
Covariance		216.05	
Correlation ($\hat{\rho}_X^2$)		0.96	

ANOVA Estimate of Reliability

ANOVA Table From Analysis of Variance of Tests 1 and 2

Source	DF	SS	MS
Person	19	8395.47	441.87
Error	20	185.50	9.27
Total	39	8580.97	

True Score Variance ($\hat{\sigma}_T^2$) 216.30 [= $(MS_p - MS_E)/n = (441.87 - 9.27)/2$]

Error Variance ($\hat{\sigma}_E^2$) 9.27 (= MS_E)

Reliability Estimate
$$(\hat{\rho}_X^2) = \frac{\hat{\sigma}_T^2}{\hat{\sigma}_T^2 + \hat{\sigma}_E^2}$$
$$= \frac{216.30}{216.30 + 9.27}$$
$$= 0.96.$$

Note that for these data, the ANOVA approach gives the same estimate of reliability (to two decimal places) as the correlational approach. It can be shown (see Lord & Novick, 1968, chap. 7) that the correlational and ANOVA approaches will be identical as long as the means of the two tests are also identical. In the present case, if the mean for Test 1 had been 105 instead of 100 (as it would have been if every score on Test 1 had 5 points added to it), then the correlational and ANOVA estimates of reliability would have diverged. The correlational estimate would be unchanged at 0.96, but the ANOVA estimate would have dropped to 0.91. Differences in test means are ignored in the correlational approach but are taken as further evidence of measurement error in the ANOVA approach.

Spearman-Brown Formula for Parallel Test Components. This formula, derived independently by C. Spearman (1910) and W. Brown (1910), is as follows:

$$\rho_X^2 = \frac{2\rho_Y^2}{1 + \rho_Y^2}, \tag{6.1}$$

where ρ_X^2 is the reliability of the composite (two-part) test and ρ_Y^2 is the reliability of either constituent part. A derivation of this formula is provided in Sidebar 6.3. The reliability coefficient of either constituent part is provided by the coefficient of correlation between the observed-score random variables for the two parts. Substitution of this part-reliability coefficient into Equation 6.1 gives the reliability of the full-length test, provided the two parts of the test are parallel. (Later, we consider what to do if the assumption of parallel parts is not plausible.) To take a concrete example, suppose that an estimate of ρ_Y^2, obtained by correlating the scores that a sample of examinees obtained on the two parts of a test, is 0.6. Then the corresponding estimate of ρ_X^2 given by Equation 6.1 is

$$\hat{\rho}_X^2 = \frac{2(0.6)}{1+0.6} = \frac{1.2}{1.6} = 0.75 .$$

The Rulon Formula and Nonparallel Test Components. If a test is composed of nonparallel parts, can the statistical information about the parts be used to obtain a coefficient of reliability for the whole? To answer this question we must pay attention to the model of true score and error that is appropriate for the test.

Suppose that the constituent parts of the test are tau-equivalent or essentially tau-equivalent. (We will relax this assumption in a moment.) This means that the true scores for a person on the test parts are either equal or they differ by an amount that is the same for each person who might be tested. (An additional aspect of tau-equivalence or essential tau-equivalence is that the standard errors of measurement for an examinee on the different test parts are neither necessarily equal nor necessarily related in a simple way.) In this situation, the following formula—first reported by the American psychometrician Philip Rulon (1939), who attributed the idea to John Flanagan, another American psychometrician—can be used to calculate the test's reliability:

$$\rho_X^2 = 2 \left[1 - \frac{(\sigma_{Y_1}^2 + \sigma_{Y_2}^2)}{\sigma_X^2} \right], \tag{6.2}$$

where $\sigma_{Y_1}^2$ and $\sigma_{Y_2}^2$ are the variances of the observed-score random variables for the two parts of the test, and σ_X^2 is the variance of the observed-score random variable for the full-length test. (See Sidebar 6.4 for a proof of this result and also of a more general result, considered two paragraphs later.)

By substituting sample estimates of $\sigma_{Y_1}^2$, $\sigma_{Y_2}^2$, and σ_X^2 in Equation 6.2, we can obtain an estimate the reliability of observations on random variable X. Consider again the test data presented in Sidebar 6.2. Suppose in this example that "Test 1" is now "Part 1" and "Test 2" is "Part 2," so the total test is now the sum of Parts 1 and 2. The Part 1 variable, which we represent here as Y_1, has an estimated variance of 227.71; the Part 2 variable Y_2 has an estimated variance of 209.96; and the total test variable X, where $X = Y_1 + Y_2$, has an estimated variance of 869.77. Substituted into Equation 6.2 as estimates of $\sigma_{Y_1}^2$, $\sigma_{Y_2}^2$, and σ_X^2, respectively, the foregoing numbers yield 0.99 as the estimate of ρ_X^2. This estimate of ρ_X^2 is considerably larger than either of the estimates of the reliability coefficient given in Sidebar 6.2. The reason is that in Sidebar 6.2 we were estimating the reliability of either Test 1 or Test 2, but here we have estimated the reliability of a composite instrument, for which Tests 1 and 2 are the constituent parts. That is, the figures reported in Sidebar 6.2 are for a test one-half as long as the test considered here. The effect of test length on reliability is studied in more detail in Chapter 7.

A feature of Rulon's formula is that it gives the reliability of the full-length test, under the specified assumptions. No correction for length is required, as in the case of the coefficient of correlation between parallel components of the test. Rulon's formula also estimates the reliability of a full-length test under the more stringent assumption of parallel components.

What if the parts of a test are neither parallel nor tau-equivalent nor essentially tau-equivalent? It is then possible to show for this situation that Rulon's formula (Equation 6.2) gives a *lower bound* to the reliability of the test. (This assertion is also proven in Sidebar 6.4.) So, use of Rulon's formula in the worst-case situation in which the test parts are neither parallel nor tau-equivalent nor essentially tau-equivalent provides a lower bound to the test's reliability coefficient. To reiterate: Rulon's formula gives the reliability coefficient for the full-length test if the test parts are parallel or tau-equivalent or essentially tau-equivalent. Otherwise, Rulon's formula gives a lower bound to reliability. Of course, the closer to 1 the number computed using Rulon's formula is, the less uncertainty there is about the test's reliability; aside, that is, from the uncertainty due to the sampling variability of the estimate. This is true even when the test components are neither parallel nor tau-equivalent nor essentially tau-equivalent.

Sidebar 6.3

A DERIVATION OF THE SPEARMAN-BROWN FORMULA

The objective is to derive the Spearman-Brown formula for the coefficient of reliability, say ρ_X^2, for a test of full length, given the coefficient of reliability, say ρ_Y^2, for a test one-half as long. To begin, we assume (1) that there exist two parallel half-length tests, and (2) that an observation on the variable Y_i for the ith half-length test is composed of true and error scores, and can be written as follows:

$$Y_{ip} = \tau_{ip} + E_{ip} \tag{6.3.1}$$

for all persons p ($p = 1, 2, 3, \ldots$) and half-length tests i ($i = 1, 2$). Because the half-length tests are parallel, it follows that

$$\tau_{1p} = \tau_{2p} \tag{6.3.2}$$

and

$$\sigma_{E_{1p}}^2 = \sigma_{E_{2p}}^2 \tag{6.3.3}$$

for all persons p. As previously noted, it follows from these assumptions that

$$\sigma_{Y_1}^2 = \sigma_{Y_2}^2 = \sigma_Y^2 \tag{6.3.4}$$

and

$$\sigma_{Y_1 Y_2} = \sigma_{T_Y}^2 . \tag{6.3.5}$$

Given Equations 6.3.4 and 6.3.5, plus the definition of reliability developed earlier, the reliability of either half-length test, say ρ_Y^2, is given by the coefficient of linear correlation between the observed-score random variables for the pair of half-length tests:

$$\rho_Y^2 = \rho_{Y_1 Y_2} = \frac{\sigma_{Y_1 Y_2}}{\sigma_{Y_1} \sigma_{Y_2}} = \frac{\sigma_{T_Y}^2}{\sigma_Y^2} . \tag{6.3.6}$$

Now form composite variables from the observed- and true-score variables of Y_1 and Y_2 as follows:

$$X = Y_1 + Y_2 \tag{6.3.7}$$

Kuder-Richardson Formula 20 and Coefficient Alpha. When a test consists of a number of items, the information contained in the item scores can be used to estimate either the reliability of the test scores or a lower-bound to their reliability. Formulas from Kuder and Richardson

---

Sidebar 6.3 Continued

and

$$T_X = T_{Y_1} + T_{Y_2}$$

$$= 2T_Y,\qquad (6.3.8)$$

the latter part of Equation 6.3.8 following from the fact that the half-test variables are parallel. Using a basic result of elementary statistics for the variance of a variable that is the sum of two other variables, and noting the results in Equations 6.3.4 and 6.3.6, we can write

$$\sigma_X^2 = \sigma_{Y_1}^2 + \sigma_{Y_2}^2 + 2\sigma_{Y_1}\sigma_{Y_2}\rho_{Y_1Y_2}$$

$$= 2\sigma_Y^2(1 + \rho_Y^2).\qquad (6.3.9)$$

Moreover, it follows from Equation 6.3.8 that

$$\sigma_{T_X}^2 = 4\sigma_{T_Y}^2.\qquad (6.3.10)$$

Using the results given in Equations 6.3.9 and 6.3.10, the reliability coefficient ρ_X^2 may be expressed as follows:

$$\rho_X^2 = \frac{\sigma_{T_X}^2}{\sigma_X^2} = \frac{4\sigma_{T_Y}^2}{2\sigma_Y^2(1 + \rho_Y^2)}.\qquad (6.3.11)$$

If we divide the numerator and denominator of Equation 6.3.11 by $2\sigma_Y^2$ and take note again of the result given in Equation 6.3.6, we obtain

$$\rho_X^2 = \frac{2\rho_Y^2}{1 + \rho_Y^2} = \frac{2\rho_{Y_1Y_2}}{1 + \rho_{Y_1Y_2}}.\qquad (6.3.12)$$

This is the Spearman-Brown formula.

(1937), Guttman (1945), and Cronbach (1951) can serve this purpose. We begin with the work of Kuder and Richardson, who focused on a test composed of dichotomously scored items (e.g., 1 for correct, 0 for incorrect). Of several equations in the Kuder–Richardson paper, the

(text continued on page 86)

Sidebar 6.4

A DERIVATION OF THE RULON FORMULA (EQUATION 6.2)

The objective here is to provide an algebraic justification of the result stated in Equation 6.2. We begin by assuming

$$Y_{1p} = \tau_{1p} + E_{1p}$$

and

$$Y_{2p} = \tau_{2p} + E_{2p}$$

for all persons p. Then

$$\sigma_{Y_1 Y_2} = \sigma_{T_1 T_2} \tag{6.4.1}$$

under the usual assumptions we make about the relationships among error and true score for random variables Y_1 and Y_2. Let

$$X_p = Y_{1p} + Y_{2p}$$

$$= \tau_p + E_p ,$$

where

$$\tau_p = \tau_{1p} + \tau_{2p} ,$$

and

$$E_p = E_{1p} + E_{2p} .$$

Then, again involving the assumptions about true- and error-score random variables, we get

$$\sigma_T^2 = \sigma_{T_1}^2 + 2\sigma_{T_1 T_2} + \sigma_{T_2}^2 \tag{6.4.2}$$

and

$$\sigma_E^2 = \sigma_{E_1}^2 + \sigma_{E_2}^2 . \tag{6.4.3}$$

Now, a coefficient of correlation cannot exceed 1 in absolute value, so we can write the following algebraic statement:

$$|\rho_{T_1 T_2}| \leq 1. \tag{6.4.4}$$

Given the definition of the coefficient of correlation $[\rho_{T_1 T_2} = (\sigma_{T_1 T_2}/\sigma_{T_1}\sigma_{T_2})]$, Equation 6.4.4 implies that

$$|\sigma_{T_1 T_2}| \leq \sigma_{T_1}\sigma_{T_2} . \tag{6.4.5}$$

Furthermore, the squared difference between the standard deviations of true-score random variables T_1 and T_2 must be nonnegative. That is,

Sidebar 6.4 Continued

$$[\sigma_{T_1} - \sigma_{T_2}]^2 \geq 0. \qquad (6.4.6)$$

Expanding the left-hand side of Equation 6.4.6 gives us

$$\sigma_{T_1}^2 - 2\sigma_{T_1}\sigma_{T_2} + \sigma_{T_2}^2 \geq 0.$$

So

$$\sigma_{T_1}^2 + \sigma_{T_2}^2 \geq 2\sigma_{T_1}\sigma_{T_2}, \qquad (6.4.7)$$

which, after using 6.4.5 and 6.4.1, we can write as

$$\sigma_{T_1}^2 + \sigma_{T_2}^2 \geq |2\sigma_{Y_1 Y_2}|$$

$$\geq 2\sigma_{Y_1 Y_2}. \qquad (6.4.8)$$

(The absolute value sign can be dropped from the term $2\sigma_{Y_1 Y_2}$ because if the left-hand side of Equation 6.4.8 is greater than the absolute value of $2\sigma_{Y_1 Y_2}$, then it must be greater than $2\sigma_{Y_1 Y_2}$ regardless of the algebraic sign of the latter term.)

By definition

$$\rho_X^2 = \frac{\sigma_T^2}{\sigma_X^2}, \qquad (6.4.9)$$

so taking the result given for σ_T^2 in Equation 6.4.2 and substituting it in Equation 6.4.9 gives

$$\rho_X^2 = \frac{\sigma_{T_1}^2 + 2\sigma_{T_1 T_2} + \sigma_{T_2}^2}{\sigma_X^2}. \qquad (6.4.10)$$

After incorporating the results of Equations 6.4.5, 6.4.7, and 6.4.8 in Equation 6.4.10, and making some algebraic manipulations, we obtain

$$\rho_X^2 \geq \frac{4\sigma_{T_1 T_2}}{\sigma_X^2} = \frac{4\sigma_{Y_1 Y_2}}{\sigma_X^2} = 2\left[\frac{\sigma_X^2 - (\sigma_{Y_1}^2 + \sigma_{Y_2}^2)}{\sigma_X^2}\right],$$

and so

$$\rho_X^2 \geq 2\left[1 - \frac{(\sigma_{Y_1}^2 + \sigma_{Y_2}^2)}{\sigma_X^2}\right],$$

which is Rulon's formula. This inequality will be a strict equality when $\rho_{T_1 T_2} = 1$ and $\sigma_{T_1} = \sigma_{T_2}$. The latter conditions hold if the variables Y_1 and Y_2 are produced by parallel or tau-equivalent or essentially tau-equivalent measures.

20th has become most widely used; its application provides what is familiarly referred to as Coefficient KR_{20}:

$$KR_{20} = \frac{n}{(n-1)} \left[1 - \frac{\sum_{i=1}^{n} \pi_i(1 - \pi_i)}{\sigma_X^2} \right], \qquad (6.3)$$

where n is the number of items in the test; π_i is the expected value (mean) of the observed-score random variable for the ith item, that is, π_i is equivalent to the proportion of examinees in the population who will answer the ith dichotomously-scored item correctly; $(1 - \pi_i)$ is the proportion of examinees who will answer the item incorrectly; and σ_X^2 is the variance of the observed-score random variable for the test, where the observed-score for an examinee is the sum of n item scores. Note that $\pi_i(1 - \pi_i)$ is the variance of the observed-score random variable for the ith item, so $\sum_{i=1}^{n} \pi_i(1 - \pi_i)$ is the sum of the item variances. An example of the calculation of KR_{20} for a set of test data is provided in Sidebar 6.5.

Various psychometricians have explored the conditions under which Equation 6.3 provides an estimate of the reliability of the measurements made of a population of examinees using a test. A theoretically satisfying study was conducted by Novick and Lewis (1967). According to their analysis, the conditions are those that must hold for the Rulon formula—the test items must be parallel or tau-equivalent or essentially tau-equivalent if KR_{20} is to estimate the ratio of true-score variance to observed-score variance for a test. It is impossible for these conditions to hold for tests in which the expected values of the random variables for the items—these are the numbers π_i ($i = 1, 2, \ldots, n$)—vary from one item to another. In most applications, therefore, Equation 6.3 estimates a lower bound to the reliability of a test. (This was proven by Novick & Lewis, 1967.)

In 1951, Lee Cronbach published what has proven to be a highly influential paper. In the paper, entitled "Coefficient Alpha and the Internal Structure of Tests," Cronbach proposed using the following formula to estimate the reliability of test data:

$$\alpha = \frac{n}{(n-1)} \left[1 - \frac{\sum_{i=1}^{n} \sigma_{Y_i}^2}{\sigma_X^2} \right]. \qquad (6.4)$$

In Equation 6.4, Coefficient α (alpha) is the index pertaining to reliability, n is the number of parts of the test, $\sigma_{Y_i}^2$ is the variance of the observed-score random variable for the ith part of the test, and σ_X^2 is the variance of the observed-score random variable for the total test. (An examinee's total test score is the sum of his or her scores on all the parts.) It is apparent that Equation 6.4 is a direct analogue of Equation 6.3 for Coefficient KR_{20}, but the test components to which Equation 6.4 applies are not restricted to being dichotomously scored items. Thus Coefficient α is a generalization of Coefficient KR_{20} to situations in which the part scores for a test are measurements on more or less continuous scales. As with Coefficient KR_{20}, Coefficient α will be equal to the reliability of a test only if the parts are parallel or tau-equivalent or essentially tau-equivalent, otherwise it gives a number that can be interpreted as a lower bound to reliability.

Other Lower Bounds to Reliability. Although Cronbach's paper on Coefficient α appeared in 1951, the coefficient itself, but not the name, had been defined earlier by Louis Guttman (1945). In fact, Guttman defined three coefficients, L_1, L_2, and L_3, of which L_3 is the formal equivalent of Coefficient α. Guttman demonstrated that these coefficients estimate lower bounds to reliability, even when no assumptions are made about the nature of the relationship among the parts of a test. The simplest of the coefficients, L_1, is defined as follows:

$$L_1 = 1 - \frac{\sum\limits_{i=1}^{n} \sigma_i^2}{\sigma_X^2}, \qquad (6.5)$$

where the terms of Equation 6.5 are defined as before. A demonstration that L_1 is a lower bound to reliability is provided in Sidebar 6.6. The value of L_1 for the mathematics test data considered in Sidebar 6.5 is 0.717, to be compared with the value of KR_{20} for the same data, 0.738.

The best of Guttman's lower bounds is L_2, which is defined as

$$L_2 = 1 - \frac{\sum\limits_{i=1}^{n} \sigma_{Y_i}^2}{\sigma_X^2} + \frac{\sqrt{\dfrac{n}{(n-1)} \sum\limits_{i=1}^{n}\sum\limits_{j=1\ (i \neq j)}^{n} \sigma_{Y_i Y_j}^2}}{\sigma_X^2}, \qquad (6.6)$$

Sidebar 6.5

DEMONSTRATING THE CALCULATION OF KR$_{20}$ FOR A SET OF TEST DATA

The test data considered here were obtained in an administration of a 36-item multiple-choice test of mathematics to 498 senior secondary-school students. The results in the following table include, for each dichotomously scored item, the sample mean score (also referred to as the proportion correct, or $\hat{\pi}$-value) and the sample variance [computed from the item mean as $\hat{\pi}(1 - \hat{\pi})$], and for the distribution of scores on the total test, the mean and variance for the sample, and finally, the KR$_{20}$ coefficient.

Item	Mean	Variance
1	0.805	0.157
2	0.554	0.248
3	0.843	0.132
4	0.380	0.236
5	0.586	0.243
6	0.763	0.181
7	0.823	0.146
8	0.275	0.200
9	0.765	0.180
10	0.896	0.094
11	0.299	0.210
12	0.550	0.248
13	0.926	0.069
14	0.114	0.102
15	0.667	0.223
16	0.516	0.250
17	0.715	0.204

---

where the new term, $\sigma^2_{Y_i Y_j}$ is the squared covariance between the observed-score random variables for the pair of test-parts i and j ($i, j = 1, 2, \ldots, n$; $i \neq j$), and $\sum_{i=1}^{n} \sum_{j=1\,(i \neq j)}^{n} \sigma^2_{Y_i Y_j}$ is the sum of squared covariance terms between the random variables for all possible pairs of test parts (i.e., for all possible combinations of the subscripts i and j such that i is not equal to j). It is possible to prove (see Sidebar 6.7) that L_2 is either larger than or equal to Coefficient α. Although Equation 6.6 makes for awkward computations in that it requires calculating the sum of squared covariance terms, the difficulty this poses is trivial if the calculations are done by computer. For the mathematics test considered in Sidebar 6.5, the value of L_2 is 0.744, in this case only slightly larger than L_3 (or KR$_{20}$), at 0.738, but larger nonetheless.

Sidebar 6.5 Continued		
18	0.452	0.248
19	0.757	0.184
20	0.359	0.231
21	0.671	0.221
22	0.514	0.250
23	0.446	0.248
24	0.723	0.201
25	0.269	0.197
26	0.261	0.193
27	0.373	0.234
28	0.213	0.168
29	0.532	0.249
30	0.341	0.225
31	0.187	0.152
32	0.211	0.167
33	0.498	0.250
34	0.412	0.243
35	0.243	0.184
36	0.060	0.057
Total Test	18.000	24.873

$$\sum_{i=1}^{n} \hat{\pi}_i (1 - \hat{\pi}_i) = 7.027$$

$$KR_{20} = \frac{36}{(36-1)} \left[1 - \frac{7.027}{24.873} \right] = 0.738$$

Why, then, is α the coefficient invariably produced by computer programs designed to inform test developers and test evaluators? The only explanation we can think of is force of habit. Before the ready availability of computing power, the calculation of L_2 would have daunted all but the most diligent and energetic of researchers. Perhaps the next generation of test developers will calculate L_2 as routinely as they now calculate Coefficient α.

A final point about the coefficients L_1, L_2, and coefficients α and KR_{20}. The computed values of these coefficients will not necessarily be greater than zero. Given a situation in which the sum of the covariances among the components of a test are negative, each of these coefficients

(text continued on page 94)

Sidebar 6.6

A Demonstration That L_1 Estimates a Lower Bound to Reliability

By definition, the reliability of the test that yields observations on the observed-score random variable X is

$$\rho_X^2 = \frac{\sigma_T^2}{\sigma_X^2},$$

where, according to the usual assumptions of classical reliability theory, the pth observation of the random variable is characterized as follows:

$$X_p = \tau_p + E_p,$$

and the variances of the random variables X, T, and E are related as follows:

$$\sigma_X^2 = \sigma_T^2 + \sigma_E^2.$$

Now suppose the test is composed of n distinct parts, so that the variable X can be viewed as the linear composite of the n variables for the test parts, say Y_j, one for each test part. Then the pth observation of random variable X can be written as follows:

$$X_p = \sum_{i=1}^{n} Y_{ip}.$$

If we can write

$$Y_{ip} = \tau_{ip} + E_{ip},$$

for the variable for each part i of the test ($i = 1, 2, \ldots, n$), then, again by the usual assumptions of classical reliability theory,

$$\sigma_{Y_i}^2 = \sigma_{T_i}^2 + \sigma_{E_i}^2 \qquad (6.6.1)$$

and

$$\sigma_{Y_i Y_j} = \sigma_{T_i T_j}. \qquad (6.6.2)$$

Consider now the n-by-n variance-covariance matrix for the variables Y_i ($i = 1, \ldots, n$). This matrix can be written as follows:

$$\Xi = \begin{pmatrix} \sigma_{Y_1}^2 & \sigma_{Y_1 Y_2} & \sigma_{Y_1 Y_3} & \cdots & \sigma_{Y_1 Y_n} \\ \sigma_{Y_2 Y_1} & \sigma_{Y_2}^2 & \sigma_{Y_2 Y_3} & \cdots & \sigma_{Y_2 Y_n} \\ \sigma_{Y_3 Y_1} & \sigma_{Y_3 Y_2} & \sigma_{Y_3}^2 & \cdots & \sigma_{Y_3 Y_n} \\ \cdots & \cdots & \cdots & \cdots & \cdots \\ \sigma_{Y_n Y_1} & \sigma_{Y_n Y_2} & \sigma_{Y_n Y_3} & \cdots & \sigma_{Y_n}^2 \end{pmatrix}.$$

Sidebar 6.6 Continued

We can see that matrix Ξ is square, containing as many rows as it has columns, namely n of each. The contents of the cells of the matrix form a pattern. The n cells of the so-called main diagonal—these are the cells in the straight line from the upper left corner to the lower right corner of the matrix—contain the variances of the variables Y_i ($i = 1, 2, \ldots, n$). The off-diagonal cells, both above and below the main diagonal, each contain a covariance between two of the Y-variables, those defined by the row and column numbers of the cell being considered. Inasmuch as there are n diagonal cells in matrix Ξ, there must be $n^2 - n = n(n - 1)$ off-diagonal cells or covariance terms. It can be shown that σ_X^2, the variance of random variable $X = \sum_{i=1}^{n} Y_i$, is the sum of all n^2 terms in matrix Ξ. Using the results in Equations 6.6.1 and 6.6.2, we see that σ_T^2 is the sum of all the off-diagonal elements of matrix Ξ plus the sum of the true-score variance components $\sigma_{T_i}^2$ of the diagonal elements of the matrix. But the true-score variance components of Equation 6.6.1 cannot be separated from the error components because we are not willing to assume the part-test variables Y_i ($i = 1, 2, \ldots, n$) are parallel or even tau-equivalent, and we do not have replicate measurements for each variable Y_i. It follows, therefore, that

$$\rho_X^2 = \frac{\sigma_T^2}{\sigma_X^2}$$

$$= \frac{\sigma_X^2 - \sum_{i=1}^{n} \sigma_{E_i}^2}{\sigma_X^2},$$

and because $\sigma_{E_i}^2 \leq \sigma_{Y_i}^2$, for all test parts i ($i = 1, 2, \ldots, n$),

$$\rho_X^2 \geq \frac{\sigma_X^2 - \sum_{i=1}^{n} \sigma_{Y_i}^2}{\sigma_X^2}. \qquad (6.6.3)$$

Expression 6.6.3 can be manipulated algebraically into the form

$$1 - \frac{\sum_{i=1}^{n} \sigma_{Y_i}^2}{\sigma_X^2} \equiv L_1, \qquad (6.6.4)$$

which is the first lower bound to reliability defined by Guttman (1945). Note that L_1 could equal the reliability coefficient ρ_X^2 only if the true-score variance $\sigma_{T_i}^2$ of the random variable for test part i was zero for all i ($i = 1, 2, \ldots, n$). But this restriction would mean that the covariances $\sigma_{T_i T_j}$ of the true-score random variables for test parts i and j also must be zero for all combinations of i and j ($i \neq j$). If this were true, the reliability coefficient ρ_X^2 would be trivially zero. In general, then, L_1 is a lower bound to the reliability coefficient ρ_X^2.

Sidebar 6.7

A Proof That L_2 Is Greater Than or Equal to Coefficient α

We begin by defining terms:

$$L_1 = 1 - \frac{\sum\limits_{i=1}^{n} \sigma_{Y_i}^2}{\sigma_X^2}$$

$$= \frac{\sum\limits_{i=1}^{n}\sum\limits_{j=1\,(i \neq j)}^{n} \sigma_{Y_i Y_j}}{\sigma_X^2},$$

$$L_2 = 1 - \frac{\sum\limits_{i=1}^{n} \sigma_{Y_i}^2}{\sigma_X^2} + \frac{\sqrt{\dfrac{n}{(n-1)} \sum\limits_{i=1}^{n}\sum\limits_{j=1\,(i \neq j)}^{n} \sigma_{Y_i Y_j}^2}}{\sigma_X^2},$$

and

$$\alpha = \frac{n}{(n-1)} L_1$$

where X is the observed-score random variable for the total test, equal to the linear combination of the random variables for the test parts ($X = \sum_{i=1}^{n} Y_i$), σ_X^2 is the variance of X, $\sigma_{Y_i}^2$ is the variance of Y_i ($i = 1, 2, \ldots, n$), and $\sigma_{Y_i Y_j}$ is the covariance of Y_i and Y_j ($i, j = 1, 2, \ldots, n; i \neq j$).

Now, substituting the expression for L_1 in the equation for L_2 and simplifying, we get

$$L_2 = \frac{\sum\limits_{i=1}^{n}\sum\limits_{j=1\,(i \neq j)}^{n} \sigma_{Y_i Y_j} + \sqrt{\dfrac{n}{(n-1)} \sum\limits_{i=1}^{n}\sum\limits_{j=1\,(i \neq j)}^{n} \sigma_{Y_i Y_j}^2}}{\sigma_X^2}$$

$$= \frac{\Gamma_2}{\sigma_X^2}, \qquad\qquad (6.7.1)$$

where Γ_2 is by definition the numerator of the right-hand side of Equation 6.7.1. Also, we can manipulate the expression for Coefficient α as follows:

$$\alpha = \frac{n}{(n-1)} \left(\frac{\sum\limits_{i=1}^{n}\sum\limits_{j=1\,(i \neq j)}^{n} \sigma_{Y_i Y_j}}{\sigma_X^2} \right)$$

Sidebar 6.7 Continued

$$= \frac{\dfrac{(n-1)}{(n-1)} \displaystyle\sum_{i=1}^{n}\sum_{j=1\;(i \neq j)}^{n} \sigma_{Y_i Y_j} + \dfrac{1}{(n-1)} \displaystyle\sum_{i=1}^{n}\sum_{j=1\;(i \neq j)}^{n} \sigma_{Y_i Y_j}}{\sigma_X^2}$$

$$= \frac{\displaystyle\sum_{i=1}^{n}\sum_{j=1\;(i \neq j)}^{n} \sigma_{Y_i Y_j} + \dfrac{1}{(n-1)} \displaystyle\sum_{i=1}^{n}\sum_{j=1\;(i \neq j)}^{n} \sigma_{Y_i Y_j}}{\sigma_X^2}$$

$$= \frac{\Gamma_3}{\sigma_X^2}, \tag{6.7.2}$$

where Γ_3 is by definition the numerator of the right-hand side of Equation 6.7.2. Now, from the definition of a variance, we can write the following expression for the variance of the $n(n-1)$ terms $\sigma_{Y_i Y_j}$ $(i, j = 1, 2, \ldots, n;\ i \neq j)$:

$$\sigma_{\sigma_{Y_i Y_j}}^2 = \left[\frac{\displaystyle\sum_{i=1}^{n}\sum_{j=1\;(i \neq j)}^{n} \sigma_{Y_i Y_j}^2}{n(n-1)} \right] - \left[\frac{\displaystyle\sum_{i=1}^{n}\sum_{j=1\;(i \neq j)}^{n} \sigma_{Y_i Y_j}}{n(n-1)} \right]^2. \tag{6.7.3}$$

It follows from the fact that a variance is necessarily greater than or equal to zero that the two terms on the right-hand side of Equation 6.7.3 have the following relationship:

$$\frac{1}{n(n-1)} \sum_{i=1}^{n}\sum_{j=1\;(i \neq j)}^{n} \sigma_{Y_i Y_j}^2 \geq \frac{1}{n^2(n-1)^2} \left[\sum_{i=1}^{n}\sum_{j=1\;(i \neq j)}^{n} \sigma_{Y_i Y_j} \right]^2.$$

Multiplying both sides of this expression by n^2 and taking the square root of both sides, we obtain the result

$$\sqrt{\frac{n}{(n-1)} \sum_{i=1}^{n}\sum_{j=1\;(i \neq j)}^{n} \sigma_{Y_i Y_j}^2} \;\geq\; \frac{1}{(n-1)} \sum_{i=1}^{n}\sum_{j=1\;(i \neq j)}^{n} \sigma_{Y_i Y_j}. \tag{6.7.4}$$

Equation 6.7.4 expresses the relationship between the unique terms of Γ_2 and Γ_3. From this result it follows that

$$\Gamma_2 \geq \Gamma_3$$

and so

$$L_2 \geq \alpha.$$

will also be negative. In this event, of course, the coefficients provide useless information about test reliability, for we know that reliability can never be less than zero. What the occurrence of negative values of L_1, L_2, or Coefficient α or Coefficient KR_{20} should do is alert the test developer or test user to the fact that the parts of the test are almost certainly not measuring the same characteristic.

Summary

We have identified several conditions to bear in mind when designing reliability experiments—recruiting random samples of participants from well-defined populations, ensuring experimental independence of the multiple measurements obtained from each participant, conducting the reliability experiment according to the same procedure that will be followed in routine applications of the measuring instrument, and conducting the experiment so as to ensure the collection of at least two measurements on each participant. We also have considered two basic designs for estimating test reliability—multiple measurements obtained on different occasions, including the test-retest experiment and the alternate-forms experiment, and multiple measurements obtained on a single occasion, with the instrument consisting of two or more parts, each of which yields a separate measurement. These different designs are sensitive to different sources of extraneous variance, which can make the estimate of the standard error of measurement larger than the quantity desired, which is σ_{E_p} or σ_E. The sources of extraneous variance for the different designs are summarized in Table 6.1.

In this chapter, we also have considered the different ways that the data collected in reliability experiments can be analyzed to obtain estimates of reliability. After conducting a test-retest or alternate-forms experiment, a researcher or test user can compute a coefficient of correlation between the measurements obtained for the participants on the two occasions. This coefficient estimates the reliability of the measurements provided the two sets of measurements can be presumed to arise from parallel tests or from tests for which the true scores and error variances are linearly related for each participant. In addition, we noted (but provided no theoretical demonstration) that the scores obtained in test-retest and alternate-forms experiments can be processed using analysis of variance techniques so as to obtain estimates of true-score variance, error variance, and reliability.

TABLE 6.1 Sources of Extraneous Variance in Estimates of the Standard Error of Measurement Based on Reliability Experiments of Different Design

	Sources of Extraneous Variance
Repeated Measurements, More Than One Occasion	
Test-retest	1. Differential recall of answers on second test occasion
	2. Differential change in the characteristic(s) measured
	3. Variations in conditions of testing that differentially affect examinee performance
	4. Any other variance due to examinee-by-occasion interaction
Alternate forms	5. Sources 2, 3, and 4, plus variation due to examinee-by-content interaction
Repeated Measurements, Same Occasion	
Test-retest	6. Source 1
	7. Differential effect of fatigue due to extended testing session
	8. Variation in conditions of testing from beginning to end of extended testing session that differentially affect examinee performance
Alternate forms	9. Sources 7 and 8, plus variation due to examinee-by-content interaction
Single Test on a Single Occasion	10. Variance due to examinee-by-content interaction, plus, perhaps, differential effect of fatigue due to extended testing session.

When a single measuring instrument is administered to a group of persons on just one occasion and the instrument is divided into two independent parts, each of which yields a score for each person, information about reliability can be obtained in one of two ways, depending on which is most appropriate. If the two part-tests are parallel, the part-test scores can be correlated and the Spearman-Brown formula (Equation 6.1) can be used to estimate the coefficient of reliability for the full-length test. Rulon's formula (Equation 6.2) will estimate the reliability of a full-length test if the part-tests are parallel or tau-equivalent or essentially tau-equivalent; this formula will estimate a lower bound to reliability otherwise. In situations where the measuring instrument yields more than two scores, one of coefficients KR_{20}, α, or L_2 can be computed. These coefficients estimate the reliability of the measuring procedure provided its parts are parallel or tau-equivalent or essentially tau-equivalent, otherwise they estimate a lower bound to the reliability coefficient. The best of these lower bounds is L_2.

Exercises

6.1. Imagine that, to estimate the reliability of essay ratings, an experiment is conducted in which each of two raters judge the essays written by a sample of examinees in response to an essay question. The ratings are on a scale from 1 to 10 (inclusive). If the second rater simply copies the ratings of the first rater, the coefficient of correlation between the two sets of ratings is 1.0. This correlation coefficient is not an acceptable estimate of the reliability of the essay rating process. Why not?

6.2. Two parallel forms of a test are administered to the same examinees, with the administrations of the tests being 1 week apart. The coefficient of correlation between examinee scores on the two tests is 0.78.

(i) Identify the sources of extraneous error variance to which this experiment is sensitive.

(ii) Suppose 2 weeks had intervened between the administrations of the two test forms. Would you expect the coefficient of correlation to be greater than 0.78, less than 0.78, or about the same? Explain.

6.3. Given the scores for a sample of examinees on each of two half-tests, under which set of assumptions about these half-tests will the Rulon formula (Equation 6.2) provide an estimate of the reliability of the total test (obtained by combining the two half-tests)? Under which set of assumptions will the Rulon formula provide an estimate of a lower bound to reliability?

6.4. Consider the following variance-covariance matrix for a test composed of four parts:

Test Part	1	2	3	4
1	2.9	2.2	2.0	2.3
2	2.2	5.4	3.6	4.0
3	2.0	3.6	4.8	3.6
4	2.3	4.0	3.6	5.5

Calculate and compare estimates of lower bounds to the reliability of the total test using the formulae for Guttman's L_1, coefficient alpha (also known as Guttman's L_3), and Guttman's L_2.

Notes

1. *Pattern-marking* refers to a test-taking behavior in which an examinee responds to the questions on a multiple-choice test without attending to the content of the questions. Pattern marking would be said to have taken place, for example, if, in responding to the questions on a test composed of four-option multiple-choice items, an examinee were to mark the first response-option to every question, or, instead, were to cycle through the response options, giving the first response option as the answer to one question, the second response option as the answer to the next question, and so on, with no effort made to choose the response options that best answered the questions.

2. Counterbalancing is an issue often considered in the conduct of reliability experiments involving the use of alternate forms of tests. *Counterbalancing* means the use of an experimental design in which the participants in the experiment are divided at random into two subgroups, with one group being administered the test forms in one order (e.g., Form A on the first occasion, Form B on the second) and the other group being administered the test forms in the reverse order (Form B on the first occasion, Form A on the second). Use of this design will tell us whether practice effects, that is gains in test performance on the second occasion relative to the first, are the same for both orders (A-B vs. B-A), and whether the overall difficulty levels of the two tests are the same. (If all individuals wrote the tests in the same order, practice effects, if any, would be confounded with differences in test difficulty.) The important point to note here is that, because order and difficulty are main effects, and so are presumed to affect all examinees equally, they can be ignored in estimating the standard error of measurement for the tests.

3. An assumption maintained throughout the present discussion is that the test can be divided into equivalent parts, as determined, for example, by number of items per part, time required to work each part, or maximum number of marks assigned per part. Theory and procedures have been developed for nonequivalent parts, but they are not considered here. See Feldt and Brennan (1989) for a review of this work.

7

Factors Affecting the Reliability Coefficient

The reliability coefficient for a set of data is sensitive to several factors, four of which are (1) time limits, (2) test length, (3) characteristics of the test items, and, for items that elicit responses that have to be scored subjectively, (4) quality of scoring. A fifth factor considered here is the heterogeneity of the sample of examinees participating in the reliability experiment. Each of these factors is discussed in turn in this chapter.

Time Limits

Whenever single-administration experiments are conducted to estimate the reliability of a test, attention must be paid to the speed at which examinees perform the test. A test is speeded when questions appearing later in the test are not reached, hence are not attempted by examinees who work too slowly. For a speeded test, the score of a slow examinee on items appearing later in the test will depend, to some extent at least, on lack of speed in performing the test rather than lack of ability to answer the items correctly. This is acceptable if speed of performance is the characteristic to be measured or if speed of performance is a part of that characteristic, otherwise it is not.

To see the impact that speededness can have on the reliability of test scores, consider estimating reliability by means of an experiment in which a single test is administered just once, with the test subsequently being divided into two equal parts, the scores on the two parts correlated, and the Spearman-Brown formula applied. Suppose the test has $2n$ items, which are divided into two subsets, each containing n items. If the division is made on a first-n-items versus second-n-items basis, then speed will affect scores on the second part of the test more than it will scores on the first part. This means the coefficient of correlation between scores on the two test-parts will be smaller than it would be were the two test-parts equally affected by the time limit, and so the estimate of reliability also will be smaller than it would be without the effect of the time limit.

Another way of dividing the items into two subsets is on the basis of their serial position in the test, as in odd-numbered versus even-numbered items. Then the items not reached by the slow examinees either will occur with equal frequency in the odd- and even-numbered subsets of items or, if the number of not-reached items is odd, will be divided such that there is only one more not-reached item in the even-numbered subset than in the odd-numbered subset. This means, following the commonly employed method of 0/1 scoring, with not-reached items treated as though they were answered incorrectly and scored 0, that an examinee will receive the identical score of 0 on the not-reached items in each subset, whether odd-numbered or even-numbered, of the test items. This perfect correspondence of scores, even though it occurs only for slow examinees and only for items that are not reached, will tend to inflate the coefficient of correlation between the scores on the odd-numbered and even-numbered subsets of items; so this correlation coefficient will be larger than it would have been were all the examinees able to attempt all the items, answering some correctly and some incorrectly, as in a test that is not speeded. An estimate of reliability based on this coefficient of correlation will also be larger than it would have been were the test not speeded.

It follows from the foregoing analysis that the reliability of scores on tests that are intentionally speeded because quickness is at least part of the configuration of skills to be measured cannot be estimated by means of an experiment involving the timed administration of only one test. Instead, the design must involve the administration of two (or more) subtests during separately timed periods. Then speededness will independently affect the scores on each of the separately timed subtests. When there are only two subtests and they are assumed to be parallel, the scores on the subtests can be correlated, and the resulting coefficient of correlation can be corrected using the Spearman-Brown formula to obtain an estimate of the reliability of the full-length test.

Test Length

An increase in the length of a test can be expected to increase the reliability of scores on the lengthened test relative to the reliability of scores on the original, shorter measuring instrument. For example, the effect of doubling the length of a test by adding a parallel set of items is that the true-score variance of the lengthened test will be four times larger than the true-score variance of the original test, but the error variance of the lengthened test will be only two times larger than the error variance of the original test. This result is demonstrated in Sidebar 7.1. In general, when test length is increased by the addition of parallel or approximately parallel components, true-score variance increases in proportion to the *square* of the increase in test length, whereas error variance increases only in proportion to the increase in test length. It follows that if increases in test length are practicable—the increase should not be so great, for example, that examinees become too fatigued to finish the lengthened test—then it is possible to obtain measurements that are as reliable as we want them to be. What is needed is theory and procedure for deriving explicit estimates of the reliability of scores on a lengthened test from an estimate of the reliability of scores on the original instrument. Then we can see how long we need to make a test in order to achieve a desired coefficient of reliability for its scores.

The theory we need was introduced in Chapter 6 under the heading *Spearman-Brown Formula*. Although developed for situations in which the reliability of a full-length test is to be estimated from the reliability of a half-length test, the Spearman-Brown formula can be readily generalized to tests composed of any number of parts. If n is the number of parts in the complete test, all parts are parallel, and ρ_Y^2 is the coefficient of reliability of any one of the parts, then ρ_X^2, the reliability of the full-length test, is given by the formula

$$\rho_X^2 = \frac{n\rho_Y^2}{1 + (n-1)\rho_Y^2}. \tag{7.1}$$

Equation 7.1 is referred to as the *generalized Spearman-Brown formula*.

Equation 7.1 can be used to estimate the increase in test length required to achieve a desired coefficient of reliability. Suppose, for example, the reliability of a part-test is 0.4 and the desired reliability of the full-length test is at least 0.8. These numbers can be substituted in Equation 7.1 for ρ_Y^2 and ρ_X^2, respectively, and then the equation can be solved for n. In this case $n = 6$, so the full-length test would have to consist of six parallel parts to achieve the desired reliability of 0.8.

It is not necessary that the test-length factor n in Equation 7.1 be a whole number. Consequently, it is possible to use the generalized Spearman-Brown formula to estimate the reliability of a test that is shorter than the so-called part-test. For example, if n were 0.5 and ρ_Y^2 were 0.6, the expected value of ρ_X^2 for a test one-half as long as the original "part" instrument would be $(0.5 \times 0.6)/[1.0 + (0.5 - 1.0)0.6] = 0.3/0.7$, or 0.43. So we see that the Spearman-Brown formula will estimate what the reliability of a test will become if it is either lengthened by adding parts that are parallel to the original test, or shortened by subtracting some of the parallel parts of which the whole test is constructed.

Item Characteristics

The reliability of scores on a test composed of two or more items must depend somehow on characteristics of the items. In the following subsections of this chapter, we consider two indices of test items that are directly related to the reliability of test scores, the index of reliability and the index of discrimination. We also consider one index that is only indirectly related to reliability, the index of difficulty. In the present context, an item's index of difficulty is nothing more than the mean value or expected value of the observed-score random variable for the item. The discrimination index for an item is here defined to be the coefficient of correlation between the observed-score random variables for the item and the total test; this index reflects the extent to which the item variable places persons in the same relative order as does the total test variable. The index of reliability for an item is the product of the standard deviation for the observed-score random variable for the item and the discrimination index for the item. Now consider each of these indices in greater detail.

Index of Reliability and Index of Discrimination

Let us begin by considering once again the formula for Coefficient α:

$$\alpha = \frac{n}{(n-1)} \left[1 - \frac{\sum_{i=1}^{n} \sigma_{Y_i}^2}{\sigma_X^2} \right], \tag{7.2}$$

(text continued on page 104)

Sidebar 7.1

A DEMONSTRATION OF THE EFFECT OF DOUBLING TEST LENGTH ON THE
VARIANCES OF TRUE AND ERROR SCORES

Suppose that test variable X is composed of two component variables, Y_1 and Y_2, such that for person p,

$$X_p = Y_{p1} + Y_{p2} \,. \tag{7.1.1}$$

Then, according to a theorem of introductory statistics,

$$\sigma_X^2 = \sigma_{Y_1}^2 + 2\sigma_{Y_1 Y_2} + \sigma_{Y_2}^2 \,, \tag{7.1.2}$$

where the terms involving σ^2 are variances and $\sigma_{Y_1 Y_2}$ is a covariance. If the basic equation of classical reliability theory is presumed to hold for test variables X, Y_1, and Y_2, such that

$$X_p = \tau_p + E_p \,, \tag{7.1.3}$$

$$Y_{p1} = \tau_{p1} + E_{p1} \,, \tag{7.1.4}$$

and

$$Y_{p2} = \tau_{p2} + E_{p2} \,, \tag{7.1.5}$$

for all persons p in the population, then it follows (see Chapters 3 and 5) under the usual assumptions of classical reliability theory, that

$$\sigma_X^2 = \sigma_T^2 + \sigma_E^2 \,, \tag{7.1.6}$$

$$\sigma_{Y_1}^2 = \sigma_{T_1}^2 + \sigma_{E_1}^2 \,, \tag{7.1.7}$$

$$\sigma_{Y_2}^2 = \sigma_{T_2}^2 + \sigma_{E_2}^2 \,, \tag{7.1.8}$$

and

$$\sigma_{Y_1 Y_2} = \sigma_{T_1 T_2} \,. \tag{7.1.9}$$

Also, it follows from the definitions

Sidebar 7.1 Continued

$$\tau_p = \tau_{p1} + \tau_{p2} \tag{7.1.10}$$

and

$$E_p = E_{p1} + E_{p2}, \tag{7.1.11}$$

together with the usual assumptions of classical reliability theory, that

$$\sigma_T^2 = \sigma_{T_1}^2 + 2\sigma_{T_1 T_2} + \sigma_{T_2}^2, \tag{7.1.12}$$

and that

$$\sigma_E^2 = \sigma_{E_1}^2 + 2\sigma_{E_1 E_2} + \sigma_{E_2}^2$$

$$= \sigma_{E_1}^2 + \sigma_{E_2}^2, \tag{7.1.13}$$

the covariance term disappearing from Equation 7.1.13 because it is assumed that random variable E_1 is independent of random variable E_2, implying that they are uncorrelated and that $\sigma_{E_1 E_2} = 0$.

Now, the reliability of Y_i ($i = 1, 2$) is $\rho_{Y_i}^2 = \sigma_{T_i}^2 / \sigma_{Y_i}^2$, whereas the reliability of X is

$$\rho_X^2 = \frac{\sigma_T^2}{\sigma_X^2}$$

$$= \frac{\sigma_T^2}{\sigma_T^2 + \sigma_E^2}$$

$$= \frac{\sigma_{T_1}^2 + 2\sigma_{T_1 T_2} + \sigma_{T_2}^2}{(\sigma_{T_1}^2 + 2\sigma_{T_1 T_2} + \sigma_{T_2}^2) + (\sigma_{E_1}^2 + \sigma_{E_2}^2)}. \tag{7.1.14}$$

We see that if $\sigma_{T_1}^2$ is approximately equal to $\sigma_{T_2}^2$, if $\sigma_{T_1 T_2}$ is approximately equal to either $\sigma_{T_1}^2$ or $\sigma_{T_2}^2$, and if $\sigma_{E_1}^2$ is approximately equal to $\sigma_{E_2}^2$, then there should be (approximately) a fourfold increase in the variance of the true-score random variable for X relative to the true-score variance for random variable Y_1 or Y_2, but (again approximately) only a twofold increase in the variance of the error random variable for X relative to the variance of the error random variable for either Y_1 or Y_2. These results hold exactly if the tests for variables Y_1 and Y_2 are parallel. Hence, we expect ρ_X^2 to be greater than ρ_Y^2.

where, as before, n is the number of items in the test, $\sigma_{Y_i}^2$ is the variance of the observed-score random variable for item i, and σ_X^2 is the variance of the random variable for total scores on the test. Written in this way, Coefficient α is seen to be a function of (1) the variances of scores on the items composing the test and (2) the variance of scores on the total test. Now, the latter variance can be manipulated as follows:

$$\sigma_X^2 = \sigma_{XX}$$

$$= \sigma_X \left(\sum_{i=1}^{n} Y_i \right)$$

$$= \sum_{i=1}^{n} \sigma_{XY_i} . \tag{7.3}$$

Recalling the definition of a coefficient of correlation, namely $\rho_{XY_i} = \sigma_{XY}/\sigma_X\sigma_{Y_i}$, we can manipulate Equation 7.3 as follows:

$$\sigma_X^2 = \sum_{i=1}^{n} \sigma_X \sigma_{Y_i} \rho_{XY_i}$$

$$= \sigma_X \sum_{i=1}^{n} \sigma_{Y_i} \rho_{XY_i} . \tag{7.4}$$

When we divide both sides of Equation 7.4 by σ_X, we see that the standard deviation of total scores on the test can be expressed as the sum over items of the product for each item, of the standard deviation of scores for the item and the coefficient of correlation between scores for the item and scores on the total test:

$$\sigma_X = \sum_{i=1}^{n} \sigma_{Y_i} \rho_{XY_i} . \tag{7.5}$$

The product of the item standard deviation and the item-total coefficient of correlation for an item is known as the *item index of reliability.*

Considering Equations 7.2 and 7.5 together, we see that Coefficient α is a function of the indices of reliability for the items. For Coefficient α to be relatively large, the sum of the item variances in Equation 7.2—that is, the sum of the squares of the item standard deviations—must be relatively small and the sum of the item indices of reliability must be relatively large. For a given value of the standard deviation of an item, the latter conditions will be satisfied best when the item-total correlation is relatively large. Thus the hallmark of a good test item, all other things constant, is one with a relatively large item-total correlation coefficient.

In many discussions of test construction, the item-total coefficient of correlation is referred to as the index of item discrimination. This label derives from the fact that scores on items associated with relatively large item-total coefficients of correlation differentiate or discriminate among examinees in a way that is more or less congruent with the way examinees are differentiated by their total test scores.

To illustrate the use of the index of reliability, we consider again the results for a 36-item multiple-choice test, which was administered to 498 senior high-school students. Various statistics for the items are presented in Table 7.1. (Some results for these items were considered previously in the discussion of Coefficient KR_{20}. Although the developments of the preceding paragraph were cast in terms of Coefficient α, remember that, when a test is composed of dichotomously scored items, Coefficient α is equivalent to Coefficient KR_{20}.) In considering Table 7.1, note that the sum of the squares of the item standard deviations of the 36 items is 7.03. The sum of the indices of reliability is 5.01, which is the standard deviation of the total test scores. These values, when substituted into Equation 7.2 for Coefficient α, return the value 0.74.

It will be observed that 16 of the items on the mathematics test have item-total correlations less that 0.30. If these items were magically transformed, such that their item-total coefficients of correlation all became 0.30 but their standard deviations remained unchanged, then the indices of reliability for these items would all increase fractionally, pushing the sum of the indices of reliability for all 36 items to 5.36 (from 5.01). An effect of this change would be to increase Coefficient α to 0.78. An increase in the reliability coefficient of 0.04 may not seem all that substantial, but in general, any increase in reliability that is achieved with no increase in test length is desirable. Moreover, if this increase is considered from the perspective of the increase in test length that would be required in order to increase the reliability coefficient by

TABLE 7.1 Statistics Based on the Responses of 498 Senior Secondary School Students to the 36 Items in a Multiple-Choice Test of Mathematics

Item	Mean	SD	Item-Total Correlation	Index of Reliability
1	0.81	0.40	0.25	0.10
2	0.55	0.50	0.27	0.14
3	0.84	0.36	0.17	0.06
4	0.38	0.49	0.43	0.21
5	0.59	0.49	0.45	0.22
6	0.76	0.43	0.20	0.09
7	0.82	0.38	0.29	0.11
8	0.28	0.45	0.34	0.15
9	0.77	0.42	0.26	0.11
10	0.90	0.31	0.30	0.09
11	0.30	0.46	0.32	0.15
12	0.55	0.50	0.44	0.22
13	0.93	0.26	0.24	0.06
14	0.11	0.32	0.21	0.07
15	0.67	0.47	0.34	0.16
16	0.52	0.50	0.28	0.14
17	0.72	0.45	0.26	0.12
18	0.45	0.50	0.30	0.15
19	0.76	0.43	0.37	0.16
20	0.36	0.48	0.38	0.18
21	0.67	0.47	0.23	0.11
22	0.51	0.50	0.42	0.21
23	0.45	0.50	0.42	0.21
24	0.72	0.45	0.31	0.14
25	0.27	0.44	0.31	0.14
26	0.26	0.44	0.34	0.15
27	0.37	0.48	0.45	0.22
28	0.21	0.41	0.25	0.10
29	0.53	0.50	0.26	0.13
30	0.34	0.47	0.34	0.16
31	0.19	0.39	0.27	0.11
32	0.21	0.41	0.31	0.13
33	0.50	0.50	0.42	0.21
34	0.41	0.49	0.33	0.16
35	0.24	0.43	0.29	0.12
36	0.06	0.24	0.09	0.02

NOTE: The Index of Reliability for an item is the product of the item standard deviation and the item-total correlation.
Sum of Indices of Reliability for the 36 Items   5.01
Sum of the Squares of the Item Standard Deviations 7.03

this amount, we find, using Equation 7.1, that the requisite increase in test length is about 20%, in this case about eight items. Clearly, using items with larger item-total coefficients of correlation makes sense insofar as increasing test reliability is concerned.

In the foregoing discussion, it should be noted that the following several issues have been slighted.

Item Validity. One cannot simply choose the items for a test on the basis of their indices of reliability, disregarding what it is the items test. First and foremost, items must be valid; that is, they must test the characteristics they were intended to test. But when two items test ostensibly the same knowledge and skills, it makes sense to choose the item with the larger index of reliability or, failing that, the item with the larger item-total correlation coefficient.

Test Composition and Examinee Sample. It is presumed in the foregoing discussion that the item-total correlation, hence the index of reliability, of an item remains constant, regardless of the other items in the test or the sample of students administered the test. Of course this is not true. The item-total correlations reported in Table 7.1 involve the total-test scores achieved on just this collection of items by just one sample of 498 students. We would expect the item-total correlation for an item to be somewhat different if one or more of the remaining 35 items in the test were different. An item-total correlation would also be expected to change due to sampling variability if the test were administered to a different sample of students. Constructing tests by choosing items on the basis of their item-total correlations, when these correlations have been estimated in pretest experiments involving different collections of items for the total test and different samples of examinees, requires an act of faith—that the correlation of the item scores with the total test scores will be approximately the same regardless of which other items are included in the test and which other examinees respond to the test. In ongoing testing programs, past experience may reinforce this faith. Still, we can never be certain that an item will behave in an operational test as it did in a pretest experiment.

Item in Total or Not? The index of discrimination we want is that between scores on the item and scores on a criterion measure of the attribute. In practice, this criterion is often approximated by the total test score. The question then arises whether the total scores with which the item scores are correlated should be based on all the items that compose the test or all the items except for the item for which the index is being calculated. When the item is a part of the total, the coefficient of correlation (index of discrimination) for the item is biased high (positively) because scores on the item correlate perfectly with that part of the total consisting of the item itself. Sometimes another coefficient of correlation is computed, either instead of or in addition to the coefficient with the item as a part of the total. In a test of n items, this alternative coefficient is between scores on the item and total scores based on the $(n - 1)$ other items in the test. For tests that are sufficiently long (say 30 items or more), with most items having relatively large indices of discrimination (say 0.30 or more), it makes little difference whether or not the item is included in the total. When the test is relatively short, however, excluding the item from the total will reduce the estimated index of discrimination substantially,[1] and we expect the smaller index to provide a more trustworthy indication of how the item will relate to total-test variables based on other sets of items.

Index of Difficulty

Attention in the foregoing discussion has been focused on the role of the item reliability index and the item-total correlation coefficient in determining the reliability of test scores. No mention was made, however, of the item difficulty index, π_i, which ranges in value between 0 and 1 for dichotomously scored items. Although this index is not directly related to the reliability of total scores on a test, it is directly related to the mean of the distribution of total scores. For a test composed of dichotomously scored items, $\mu_X = \sum_{i=1}^{n} \pi_i$, where μ_X is the expected value of the observed-score random variable for the total test, n is the number of items in the test, and π_i is expected value of the observed-score random variable for item i ($i = 1, 2, \ldots, n$). By choosing n relatively easy items for our test, we would expect the test mean to be relatively large, coming as close to n as the items chosen have π_i values near 1. We also would expect the distribution of total scores on such a test to be negatively skewed. On the other hand, by choosing relatively difficult items, we can produce a test expected to yield a positively skewed distribution of scores, with a mean near 0 if the π-values of the items are all near 0. To have a test mean relatively near the center of the test score scale, it is necessary to choose items that, on average at least, have π-values near 0.5. Dichotomously scored items with π-values near 0.5 also will have maximum possible score variance, because the variance of the observed-score random variable for dichotomously scored item i is $\pi_i(\pi_i - 1)$, and this expression attains its maximum of 0.25 when $\pi_i = 0.5$.

Considerations of item difficulty, the location of the mean of the distribution of total test scores, and the skewness of this distribution are indirectly relevant to a discussion of the reliability of the test scores. Granted, a test composed of items that are all very easy or very difficult for the examinees to whom the test will be administered can be expected to yield relatively unreliable scores; in this case, the variance of true scores will tend to be small, so most of the variation in observed scores likely will be due to error of measurement. When the objective is to maximize reliability, it is often recommended that the items chosen for a test should be of middle difficulty; then the variation of true scores will be large if the test is capable of yielding highly reliable test scores for the examinees from a specified population. Also, if the item-total correlation coefficient is assessed using the point-biserial (Pearson product-moment) coefficient, then, other things constant, this coefficient tends to be larger when the value of π_i is relatively near 0.5 rather than when it is relatively near 1 or 0. (The point-biserial coefficient of correlation between item and total test scores is what is reported in Table 7.1.) That the items of a test are of middle difficulty is not sufficient, however, to ensure that scores on the test are highly reliable.

Quality of the Scoring of Subjectively Scored Items

The discussion to this point of this chapter has focused, not always explicitly, on items that are dichotomously scored. Very often, dichotomously scored items are in the multiple-choice format and can be objectively scored. When, however, the response to an item must be constructed by the examinee and the range of possible responses is large, then scoring requires the judgment of a scorer. To the extent that the judgments of one scorer vary unsystematically from those of another scorer, or to the extent that the judgments of just one scorer vary unsystematically over time, then the score assigned a particular response will depend on the particular individual assigned the task of scoring a response or, in the event that only one judge is involved and scoring extends over a period of time, the score will depend on the judgmental frame of reference the judge brings to bear on the response when the scoring is done. For example, experiments in which essays are rescored by the same judge, who cannot refer to the scores assigned during the first scoring, reveal considerable variation in the scores assigned to given essays, such that the coefficient of correlation between the two sets of scores is less than 1, usually considerably less. This variation in scores from one scoring occasion to the next reflects a kind of error of measurement for subjectively scored tests.

Assessing the magnitude of the variation due to intra- and inter-judge variability in the scoring of extended-response tests (as opposed to multiple-choice and other forms of objectively scored tests) requires carefully designed experiments. The kinds of experiments involved are considered in discussions of generalizability theory, a topic that is treated in another book in this series (Shavelson & Webb, 1991).

Heterogeneity of the Population of Examinees

An implication of Equation 4.1 is that, for a given variance of observed scores, the size of the coefficient of reliability depends on the magnitude of the variance of true scores. If there is no true-score variation among examinees on the attributes measured by a test, then the examinees' scores on the test will have zero reliability no matter how large the observed-score variance may be. On the other hand, examinees can be chosen so as to inflate spuriously the true-score variance, and thus to enhance the impression of reliability for the scores obtained on a test. Consider, for example, a test of some characteristic (say, size of vocabulary) that increases with the age of examinees, at least for school-age populations. Suppose a test is developed to assess the vocabulary of students in Grade 6. The variance of true scores for the vocabulary test in a population of sixth-grade students is expected to be narrower than the variance of true scores for the test in a population consisting of fifth-, sixth-, and seventh-grade students. A possibly false impression of the reliability of the scores yielded by the test can be created if the estimate of reliability is derived from an experiment in which fifth-, sixth-, and seventh-grade students are tested when, instead, the test will only be used with sixth-grade students. This is another reason why it is important, in evaluating an estimate of reliability, to consider both the nature of the examinee population that was sampled in the reliability experiment and the nature of the examinee population on which the test will be used in practice.

Summary

In this chapter we have considered several factors that can affect the reliability coefficient for a set of scores on a test. Time limit is one such factor. Whether or not the performance on which a measurement is based is speeded affects reliability, and in addition has an affect on what is measured; that is, it affects validity. Any coefficient of reliability resulting from an experiment in which a single test is administered only once to a sample of examinees can be spuriously affected by speeding, with the resulting coefficient being either too large or too small, depending on how it is calculated. The reliability of time-limited tests is best estimated by means of an experiment in which at least two separately timed tests or subtests are administered to examinees.

Another important factor affecting reliability is test length. In general, the longer the test, the more reliable the scores produced by the test will be. The generalized Spearman-Brown formula can be used to estimate the impact of a change in test length on test reliability.

The item characteristic of discrimination, typically measured by means of an "item-total" coefficient of correlation, was shown to affect the reliability of test scores. The greater the indices of discrimination for a set of items, the larger we can expect the coefficient of reliability of scores on the test to be. This expectation also holds for a derivative index, the item reliability index, which is the product of the standard deviation of scores on an item and the discrimination index for the item.

Another item characteristic, that of difficulty, is not directly related to the reliability coefficient. What item difficulty affects directly is the expected mean score on the test, and this in turn affects whether or not the test score distribution will be symmetrical or skewed. The distribution of test scores will be skewed positively if the test is composed of difficult items, and skewed negatively if the test is composed of easy items.

Two other factors affecting the reliability coefficient were considered: the quality of the scoring of subjectively scored items and the heterogeneity of the examinee population. When scoring is subjective, as opposed to objective, inconsistency in the performance of scorers will lower reliability. When the examinee population is heterogeneous in the sense that the variance of true scores among examinees is large, score reliability will also tend to be large. Ideally the sample of examinees used to estimate the reliability will be drawn from the same population of examinees as are the examinees to which the test will be applied in practice.

Exercises

7.1. The scores on a test for a population of examinees have a reliability coefficient of 0.6. What will be the expected reliability of scores if the length of the test is doubled by the addition of parallel components? tripled? halved by the subtraction of parallel components?

7.2. Consider the following table of statistics for a 13-item test. Assume the statistics are based on the responses of a large, representative sample of examinees from a well-defined population of interest to the tester.

Item	Mean	SD	Item-Total Correlation	Index of Reliability
1	0.79	0.41	0.31	0.13
2	0.79	0.41	0.49	0.20
3	0.72	0.45	0.41	0.18
4	0.69	0.46	0.56	0.26
5	0.48	0.50	0.50	0.25
6	0.45	0.50	0.62	0.31
7	0.41	0.49	0.06	0.03
8	0.41	0.49	0.48	0.24
9	0.38	0.49	0.46	0.23
10	0.38	0.49	0.40	0.20
11	0.24	0.43	0.16	0.07
12	0.17	0.38	0.30	0.11
13	0.14	0.34	0.46	0.16

(i) Identify the two weakest appearing items on the basis of these statistics. Which statistic did you use for this purpose, and why?

(ii) Identify the four items that appear to be strongest on the basis of the item-total correlation. Repeat the process using the index of reliability. What is unusual about these two sets of four items? Explain the unusual result.

Note

1. The magnitude of the item-total correlation coefficient also depends on just which kind of correlation has been calculated. Two coefficients are commonly used with dichotomously scored items: the point-biserial coefficient and the biserial coefficient. The former coefficient is simply the Pearson product-moment correlation coefficient between the item scores and the total-test scores. The biserial coefficient, although related by an explicit mathematical expression to the point-biserial coefficient, is not a Pearson product-

moment coefficient and has a different set of properties, including the fact that it is larger (in absolute value) than the point-biserial coefficient. Readers interested in learning more about the biserial coefficient and its relationship to the point-biserial coefficient should study chapter 15 of Lord and Novick (1968).

8

Estimating the Standard Error of Measurement

As we have seen in Chapter 3, a concept central to test theory is the standard error of measurement (SEM). Before we can make use of this concept, for example to define confidence intervals for true scores or to judge the significance of the difference between two observed scores, we must be able to estimate its numerical size. In this chapter we describe a procedure for obtaining a defensible estimate of the SEM for a person's test score, a quantity we have referred to previously as the person-specific standard error of measurement, or PSEM.

Review and Comments

Given an estimate of the reliability of a set of test scores, we could estimate the SEM using Equation 4.2.3:

$$\hat{\sigma}_E = \hat{\sigma}_X \sqrt{1 - \hat{\rho}_X^2} \ .$$

This estimate is not ideal, however, in that, as was observed in Sidebar 4.2, it can be interpreted as the square root of the average of the person-specific error variances of all the examinees who participated in the reliability estimation experiment. Although to know this is better than to know nothing about error of measurement, it would be preferable to know the standard deviation of the person-specific observed-score random variable for each individual examinee. (Recall that the person-specific observed-score random variable is identical, except for center or mean, to the person-specific error random variable.) This person-specific standard error of measurement (PSEM) may differ in size from one examinee to another.

The expectation that the PSEM can vary from one examinee to another follows from a simple thought experiment. Assume a test is composed of n items, with each item scored 0 or 1 (incorrect or correct), and with the total-test score equal to the simple sum of item scores. For this test, true scores can range from 0 to n, as can observed scores, although, as noted in Chapter 3, true scores can be any real number between 0 and n whereas observed scores can only be whole numbers. Now consider three examinees, one with a true score near the bottom of the true-score scale, another with a true score near the middle of the scale, and the third with a true score near the top of the scale. The examinee with the low true score is expected, on repeated testing, to obtain observed scores that are consistently low. Indeed, if the standing of this examinee is so extreme that his or her true score is 0 and if it is not possible to answer items correctly by guessing, then the observed scores of this individual, on repeated testing, will necessarily all equal 0, and his or her PSEM will be 0. That the PSEM of the examinee whose true score is at or very near the top of the true-score scale should be small follows from a similar argument. In contrast, the observed-scores of the examinee with a middling true-score have much greater potential for variation on both sides of the true score. No floor or ceiling effect can operate to reduce the potential variability of observed scores for this examinee.

Because the size of the PSEM can be expected to vary from one examinee to another, we concur with the recommendation of the *Test Standards* Committee that "standard errors of measurement should be reported at critical score levels" (Committee of AERA, APA, & NCME, 1985, Standard 2.10, p. 22). This Committee went on to acknowledge, however, that "reporting standard errors of measurement at every score level may not be feasible in some circumstances, but they should be reported at appropriate, well-separated levels or intervals" (p. 22). We consider now how this objective might be accomplished.

Some Theory for the SEM

A problem that confronts us immediately as we think about the problem of estimating the SEM for a person's test score is that his or her true score is never known. Only observed scores are available, so we must work with them, somehow, to estimate the SEM. Before we are ready do so, however, we need to review some theory.

To start, let us assume a single test of $2n$ dichotomously scored items. The number $2n$ is chosen because it is divisible by 2, so we also assume the $2n$ items are divided into two sets, each containing n items. Now we can apply classical reliability theory to define the following relationships among observed, true, and error scores for the full test of $2n$ items and the two part-tests, each of n items:

$$X_p = \tau_p + E_p, \quad \text{[Equation for full test]}$$

$$X_{1p} = \tau_{1p} + E_{1p}, \quad \text{[Equation for Part 1]}$$

$$X_{2p} = \tau_{2p} + E_{2p}, \quad \text{[Equation for Part 2]}$$

where the subscripts 1 and 2 refer to the two part-tests and the subscript p refers to the person to whom the scores apply. Other equivalences are these:

$$X_p = X_{1p} + X_{2p}, \quad \text{[The total-test score is the sum of the scores on the part-tests.]}$$

$$\tau_p = \tau_{1p} + \tau_{2p}, \quad \text{[The true score on the total test is the sum of the true scores on the part-tests.]}$$

$$E_p = E_{1p} + E_{2p}. \quad \text{[The error score on the total test is the sum of the error scores on the part-tests.]}$$

We proceed on the assumption that the two sets of items, which generate observations on the person-specific random variables X_{1p} and X_{2p}, are parallel according to the definition given in Chapter 5. (If they are not strictly parallel, then the results that follow cannot be strictly true for the test, but they may well be close enough to be useful in practice.) Given parallel parts, each person p has the same true scores and PSEMs on the two part-tests; that is, $\tau_{1p} = \tau_{2p}$, and $\sigma^2_{E_{1p}} = \sigma^2_{E_{2p}}$. Under the usual assumption that errors of measurement E_{1p} and E_{2p} are uncorrelated for any person p over repeated observations of the random variables X_{1p} and X_{2p}, it follows that

$$\sigma^2_{E_p} = \sigma^2_{E_{1p}} + \sigma^2_{E_{2p}}.$$

According to this equation, the variance for person p of observations on the error random variable for total test, $\sigma^2_{E_p}$, is the simple sum of the variances of observations on the error random variables for the two part-tests, $\sigma_{E_{1p}}^2$ and $\sigma_{E_{2p}}^2$.

Consider now the difference for person p between observed scores X_{1p} and X_{2p}. Under the assumption that the two parts of the test are parallel,

$$X_{1p} - X_{2p} = (\tau_{1p} + E_{1p}) - (\tau_{2p} + E_{2p})$$

$$= E_{1p} - E_{2p}.$$

The difference $X_{1p} - X_{2p}$ is a random variable, and so has a variance that can be seen, in the following series of equations, to equal the variance of the error random variable for person p on the total test:

$$\sigma_{(X_{1p} - X_{2p})}^2 = \sigma_{(E_{1p} - E_{2p})}^2$$

$$= \sigma_{E_{1p}}^2 + \sigma_{E_{2p}}^2$$

$$= \sigma_{E_p}^2. \tag{8.1}$$

It is shown in Sidebar 8.1 that the squared difference between an examinee's observed scores on two part-tests, say $(X_{1p} - X_{2p})^2$, is an estimate of the error variance $\sigma_{E_p}^2$ for person p. The square root of this squared difference is easily calculated to estimate the PSEM for an individual. Unfortunately, the aforementioned squared difference is statistically unreliable because it is based on only two scores, the minimum number of observations required for estimating a variance. We need to find a better estimate.

Suppose we were able to group persons by the values of their true scores τ_p. Then, on the assumption that all persons with the same true score have the same PSEM, we could compute the square root of the mean of the error-variance estimates for the individuals in each group. Granted, this average might not equal the standard deviation of the error-score random variable on the test for any individual in the group. But if this standard deviation changes size systematically along the true-score scale of the test, as we expect it to, then the square root of the mean error-variance for the members of a group with the same true score should better approximate the PSEM for any member of the group than should the square root of the mean error-variance for all persons

Sidebar 8.1

A PROOF THAT THE SQUARED DIFFERENCE BETWEEN PARALLEL
PART-TEST SCORES ESTIMATES THE PSEM

Suppose a test composed of $2n$ items has been divided into two parts, each containing n items. Let the scores of the pth examinee on the two parts be X_{1p} and X_{2p}, respectively. If it is assumed that the two part-tests are parallel, then the scores X_{1p} and X_{2p} can be viewed as two observations on the same person-specific observed-score variable. Moreover, the difference between X_{1p} and X_{2p}, under the assumption of parallel part-tests, is due only to error of measurement. This means that the variance of the difference between these two observations is an estimate of the variance of the error variable for the parallel part-tests for person p.

Consider next the algebraic expression for obtaining an estimate of the variance of variable X_p from single observations of the variables X_{1p} and X_{2p}. Because the error random variable under consideration is for part-test scores, in this instance half-test scores, we denote the estimate of variance as $\hat{\sigma}^2_{E_{1/2p}}$. In calculating this estimate, we need the mean of the observations. Inasmuch as there are only two observed scores, X_{1p} and X_{2p}, their mean is

$$\overline{X}_p = \frac{X_{1p} + X_{2p}}{2}. \tag{8.1.1}$$

It follows from the basic equation for obtaining an unbiased estimate of the variance of a random variable from two observations that

$$\hat{\sigma}^2_{E_{1/2p}} = \frac{(X_{1p} - \overline{X}_p)^2 + (X_{2p} - \overline{X}_p)^2}{(N-1)} \tag{8.1.2}$$

$$= (X_{1p} - \overline{X}_p)^2 + (X_{2p} - \overline{X}_p)^2,$$

because N, the number of observations, is 2. Substituting the right-hand side of Equation 8.1.1 for $\overline{X}_p$ in Equation 8.1.2, we get

(ignoring group membership). Unfortunately, we never know true scores, so we cannot group persons by their true scores.

A Practical but Flawed Approach

A problem besetting the estimation method outlined in the previous section, as has been noted, is that we presumed examinees can be grouped on the basis of their true scores. But the true score of an examinee can never be known, so it is senseless to continue with the

---

Sidebar 8.1 Continued

$$\hat{\sigma}^2_{E_{V_2 p}} = \left[\frac{2X_{1p} - (X_{1p} + X_{2p})}{2}\right]^2 + \left[\frac{2X_{2p} - (X_{1p} + X_{2p})}{2}\right]^2$$

$$= \left(\frac{X_{1p} - X_{2p}}{2}\right)^2 + \left(\frac{X_{2p} - X_{1p}}{2}\right)^2$$

$$= \frac{2(X_{1p} - X_{2p})^2}{4}$$

$$= \frac{d_p^2}{2},$$

where $d_p = X_{1p} - X_{2p}$ is the difference between the two part-test scores and $\hat{\sigma}^2_{E_{V_2 p}}$ is the estimated variance of scores on parallel part-tests.

According to Equation 8.1, the variance of the person-specific error random variable for a total test composed of two parallel part-tests is twice the variance of the person-specific observed-score random variable for the parallel part-tests. Equivalently, the person-specific error variance for the total test is twice the person-specific error variance for one of the parallel part-tests. It follows, then, that

$$\hat{\sigma}^2_{E_p} = 2\hat{\sigma}^2_{E_{V_2 p}} = d_p^2 = (X_{1p} - X_{2p})^2, \tag{8.1.3}$$

which is to say that the squared difference in the scores examinee p achieves on each of two parallel part-tests is an estimate of the variance of the error random variable for the test composed of both part-tests.

It is a straightforward exercise in the algebra of statistics to show that the expected value of the *estimate* of error variance provided by Equation 8.1.3 is the error variance itself. In other words, $(X_{1p} - X_{2p})^2$ is an unbiased estimate of $\hat{\sigma}^2_{E_p}$.

---

assumption that it can. Practical methods necessarily involve the use of observed scores.

A practical but flawed approach is to establish groups on the basis of observed test scores. That this approach is flawed can be seen as follows: Given a group of examinees, all of whom have the same observed score X on the $2n$ items of the total test, and given that $X = X_1 + X_2$, it follows that, for the persons in the group, there exists a negative correlation between X_1 and X_2. (Given fixed X, for every increase in X_1 there must be a corresponding decrease in X_2.) But we expect X_1 and X_2 to be uncorrelated because, for parallel part-tests, X_1 and X_2 for any person p should differ only because of the effects of measurement error. By fixing observed-score X and averaging the individual estimates of the variance of errors of measurement over examinees with this observed score, we have produced a biased estimate of the variance of errors of measurement for the subpopulation. (See Sidebar 8.2 for an algebraic demonstration of this assertion.) A better approach is outlined in the next section of this chapter.

A Better Approach

To avoid the biases described in Sidebar 8.2, Woodruff (1990) suggested the following procedure. As before, we assume a test is divisible into two parts of equal length. In the ideal case, the two parts are parallel or very nearly so. Groups are established using observed scores on the *first* part of the test. For the examinees in a group with identical scores on the first part of the test, scores on the items in the *second* part of the test are analyzed to obtain an estimate of error variance. This can be done by computing for the group, (i) the standard deviation of total scores on the *second* part of the test, (ii) Coefficient KR_{20} from their scores on the items of the *second* part of the test, and (iii) entering these statistics into Equation 4.2.3. The result is an estimated PSEM for the members of the group, with the estimated PSEM pertaining to scores in one-half the test. An estimate pertaining to total-test scores can be obtained by squaring the estimated PSEM for the half-test, doubling it, and taking the square root of the result. (These steps are indicated by the theoretical result in Equation 8.1.)

Although the estimate of error variance obtained by the foregoing method is based on only one-half the items in the test, this estimate offers the advantage that the errors of measurement that affected the grouping of examinees were excluded from the process of estimating the error variance for the group. Although the examinees in each group have the same (or very nearly the same[1]) observed scores on the half of the test used to form groups, these examinees will not necessarily have the same observed score on the other half of the test, the one used to obtain the estimates of error variance. In this way, spurious correlations between errors of measurement on the two halves of the test are avoided for the members of a subgroup.

Some results obtained using Woodruff's approach to estimating the standard error of measurement are given in Table 8.1. The data used in this demonstration were the responses of 498 senior high-school students to a 36-item multiple-choice test of mathematics. (Some item statistics for this test were reported earlier in Table 7.1.) The test was divided into two 18-item part-tests, the odd-numbered items forming one part-test, the even-numbered items forming the other part-test. These two test parts are not parallel for these examinees, in that the mean scores on the two parts are not equal (10.4 for the part of odd-numbered items, 7.6 for the part of even-numbered items), but their variances are very nearly equal (7.87 for odd, 7.88 for even). The correlation coefficient between scores on the two parts is 0.58, indicating that the reliability of the part-scores is relatively low.

As for the results reported in Table 8.1, the variability among the estimates of SEM by test-score level is not great. Still, the tendency is for estimates of the SEM to be larger for scores in the middle of the score scale than for scores at the extremes. Relatively few examinees received extreme scores. Consequently, the estimates of error variance for the lowest and highest score categories were derived by combining the examinees whose scores on the test-part consisting of the odd-numbered items covered six (lowest) and four (highest) adjacent score categories respectively.

Summary

This chapter addressed the matter of estimating the standard error of measurement (SEM) for an examinee's test score. The SEM is expected to differ, depending on the magnitude of a person's true score; it should be larger for persons with true scores in the middle of the test score scale, and smaller for persons with true scores at the extremes of the test score scale. Equation 4.2.3 is unsatisfactory because it estimates an average value of the SEM, the average being taken over all the persons involved in the experiment, not just those with a specified true score.

To estimate the PSEM for a person, it was shown that all that is required is observed scores on two parallel, or approximately parallel, part-tests; the squared difference between these observed scores estimates the squared PSEM of the person. But this estimate is statistically unstable, being based on only two observations. Better estimates require grouping individuals somehow, according to expected true-score level, and obtaining an average SEM for each different group.

It was shown that a good way to group persons is on the basis of their observed scores on Part 1 of a test. Then an average SEM can be

(text continued on page 124)

Sidebar 8.2

A DEMONSTRATION THAT GROUPING EXAMINEES BY TOTAL TEST SCORES
GIVES BIASED ESTIMATES OF PSEMs

We start from the same assumptions as were made in Sidebar 8.1. The estimate of
error variance for person p that is given in Equation 8.1.2 is

$$\hat{\sigma}^2_{E_p} = 2\hat{\sigma}^2_{E_{V_{2p}}} = d^2_p = (X_{1p} - X_{2p})^2 .$$

Taking the mean of $\hat{\sigma}^2_{E_p}$ over the N_g examinees composing group g, all members of
which group have identical observed scores $X_g = X_1 + X_2$, we obtain the following
expression:

$$\hat{\sigma}^2_{E_g} = \frac{\displaystyle\sum_{p=1}^{N_g} \hat{\sigma}^2_{E_p}}{N_g} \tag{8.2.1}$$

where N_g is the size of group g (for which observed scores on the test are fixed at X_g
$= X_1 + X_2$). Expanding Equation 8.2.1 using the results in Equation 8.1.2, we obtain
the following result:

$$\hat{\sigma}^2_{E_g} = \frac{\displaystyle\sum_{p=1}^{N_g} (X_{1p} - X_{2p})^2}{N_g}$$

$$= \frac{\displaystyle\sum_{p=1}^{N_g} (X^2_{1p} + X^2_{2p} - 2X_{1p}X_{2p})}{N_g} \tag{8.2.2}$$

$$= \frac{(N_g - 1)}{N_g} \hat{\sigma}^2_{X_{1g}} + \overline{X}^2_{1g} + \frac{(N_g - 1)}{N_g} \hat{\sigma}^2_{X_{2g}} + \overline{X}^2_{2g} - \frac{2(N_g - 1)}{N_g} \hat{\sigma}_{X_{1g}X_{2g}} - 2\overline{X}_{1g}\overline{X}_{2g} .$$

The results given in Equation 8.2.2 follow in part from the formula for estimating the
variance of a random variable from sample data, namely

$$\hat{\sigma}^2_X = \frac{N}{(N-1)} \left[\frac{\displaystyle\sum_{p=1}^{N} X^2_p}{N} - \overline{X}^2 \right],$$

which implies

Sidebar 8.2 Continued

$$\frac{\sum\limits_{p=1}^{N} X_p^2}{N} = \frac{(N-1)}{N} \hat{\sigma}_X^2 + \overline{X}^2 .$$

Also,

$$\hat{\sigma}_{X_1 X_2} = \frac{N}{(N-1)} \left[\frac{\sum\limits_{p=1}^{N} X_{1p} X_{2p}}{N} - \overline{X}_1 \overline{X}_2 \right] ,$$

so

$$\frac{\sum\limits_{p=1}^{N} X_{1p} X_{2p}}{N} = \frac{(N-1)}{N} \hat{\sigma}_{X_1 X_2} + \overline{X}_1 \overline{X}_2 .$$

If the means of the random variables for the two part-tests are equal, then we can expect $\overline{X}_1$ and $\overline{X}_2$ to be nearly equal for group g; in this case Equation 8.2.2 reduces to

$$\hat{\sigma}_{E_g}^2 = \frac{(N_g - 1)}{N_g} (\hat{\sigma}_{X_{1g}}^2 + \hat{\sigma}_{X_{2g}}^2 - 2\hat{\sigma}_{X_{1g} X_{2g}}) . \tag{8.2.3}$$

By the argument advanced in the text, $\hat{\sigma}_{X_{1g} X_{2g}}$ is expected to be negative in group g, which means that $\hat{\sigma}_{E_g}^2$, as given by Equation 8.2.1, should be larger than it would be if the covariance $\hat{\sigma}_{X_{1g} X_{2g}}$ were zero, as the covariance between independent errors of measurement should be. [If the part-test means are not equal, as assumed in going from Equation 8.2.2 to Equation 8.2.3, the effect on $\hat{\sigma}_{E_g}^2$ is to make it larger than it would be, were the means equal. The reason is that in general $(\overline{X}_{1g}^2 + \overline{X}_{2g}^2) \geq 2\overline{X}_{1g} \overline{X}_{2g}$, with equality only when $\overline{X}_{1g} = \overline{X}_{2g}$.]

In a study of $\sigma_{E_g}^2$, Woodruff (1990) demonstrated that the expected value of $\sigma_{E_g}^2$ over groups formed on the basis of observed test scores X must be *less* than the expected value of $\sigma_{E_g}^2$ over groups formed on the basis of true test scores τ. The relationship described by Woodruff is opposed to that described in the preceding paragraph. These two effects might offset one another, at least partially. But it would be preferable to employ an unbiased estimator of $\sigma_{E_g}^2$. Just such an estimator is described in the section "A Better Approach" of this Chapter.

TABLE 8.1 Estimates of the SEM at Several Levels of Achievement Using Woodruff's Method

Score on Part-Test (Odd-Numbered Items)	Frequency	Estimated Score on Total Test*	Estimated SEM for Total Test (Derived from Responses to Even-Numbered Items)
1-6	44	1-10	2.4
7	30	12	2.5
8	50	14	2.5
9	56	16	2.5
10	74	17	2.5
11	62	19	2.6
12	67	21	2.6
13	49	23	2.7
14	33	24	2.5
15-18	33	26-32	2.5

NOTE: See text for a description of Woodruff's method.

* The estimated total-test score is a linear transformation of the scale for the part-test of 18 odd-numbered items. The transformation turns the distribution of scores on this part-test into a distribution with the same mean and standard deviation as the distribution of scores on the full 36-item test. (Given that the mean and standard deviation of the distribution of scores on the full test were 18.00 and 4.99, respectively, and on the half-test consisting of odd-numbered items were 10.40 and 2.81, respectively, the transformation was

$$\hat{X}_{Total} = \frac{4.99}{2.81}(X_{Odd} - 10.40) + 18.00$$

$$= 1.78 X_{Odd} - 0.51.$$

So, for example, given a score X_{Odd} of 8, the estimated score for X_{Total} is 13.73, which is rounded to 14 because observed total-test scores must be whole numbers.

calculated for each group from their observed scores on the items of Part 2 of the test.

Exercises

8.1. A test has been divided into parallel half-tests. An examinee achieves scores of 10 and 13 on the two half-tests. What do you estimate the personal standard error of estimate (PSEM) to be for this examinee?

8.2. (i) Using information from Table 7.1, compute an estimate of the average SEM for the mathematics test. (Hint: Compute the statistics you need to apply Equation 4.2.3.)

(ii) Compare the average SEM you just computed with the estimates of PSEMs given in Table 8.1 for the same test. Use the width of the confidence interval for the true score as the basis of your comparison.

Note

1. If the total sample of examinees is relatively small, it may be necessary, particularly in the tails of the distribution of observed scores on the first part of the test, to combine several subgroups with adjacent scores in order to produce a subgroup large enough to yield a statistically satisfactory estimate of error variance.

9

Special Topics Involving Reliability

In this chapter we consider two special topics. One of these topics is the measurement of growth or change. The conception of reliability we have been employing thus far, specifically the conception rooted in the notion of consistency, has been studied extensively in the context of measuring change, and we explore here some of the results of these studies. The other special topic involves so-called criterion-referenced measurement. We consider how this kind of measurement differs from norm-referenced measurement, and see that it is sometimes useful to conceptualize reliability in the context of criterion-referenced measurement somewhat differently from the way the notion of reliability has been developed heretofore.

Reliability of Difference Scores

When one thinks of measuring change in the height of a child, the procedure seems straightforward: Height in inches is measured as the distance from floor to top of head as the child stands with feet flat on the floor and body erect. The procedure is repeated several weeks or months later, and change is recorded as the difference between the first and second measurements. In this way we can define a random variable, observations of which consist of measurements of the change in the height of a particular child. It would then be natural to consider certain features of this random variable, for example its mean and variance, when assessing whether or not the child's height had increased during the interval between the first and second measurements.

In the present discussion, our focus is on the consistency of measurements of change in the heights of children. As before, the consistency referred to is that associated with the repeated measurement experiment, but the experiment is now more complicated. It involves obtaining multiple readings of the *change-score* random variable for a person. The person-specific standard error of measurement for change would tell us what we would like to know about the measurement of change for an individual. For a group, we might instead concentrate our attention on the reliability of the difference scores for the individuals in the group.

Simple Difference Scores

The simplest measure of change, the one suggested in the foregoing discussion of growth in the height of children, is the difference between the measurements obtained on the first and second measurement occasions. To symbolize this difference, we let X_p represent the initial or premeasurement for person p of the characteristic of interest, and we let Y_p represent a subsequent postmeasurement. Then we define D_p to be the change or difference score for person p:

$$D_p = Y_p - X_p , \quad (p = 1, 2, 3, \ldots). \tag{9.1}$$

It follows from Equation 9.1 and a basic theorem of statistics, which we have used before, that the variance of the random variable D_p, say σ_D^2, as a function of the variances of the random variables Y_p and X_p and their covariance, is as follows:

$$\sigma_D^2 = \sigma_Y^2 + \sigma_X^2 - 2\sigma_{YX} . \tag{9.2}$$

If classical test theory is invoked for the observed pre- and postmeasures, X_p and Y_p, then it follows that D_p also can be expressed as the sum of true and error difference scores:

$$D_p = (\tau_{Y_p} + E_{Y_p}) - (\tau_{X_p} + E_{X_p})$$

$$= (\tau_{Y_p} - \tau_{X_p}) + (E_{Y_p} + E_{X_p})$$

$$= \tau_{D_p} + E_{D_p} . \tag{9.3}$$

Expressions for the variances of the true-score and error-score parts of the difference-score variable are as follows:

$$\sigma_{T_D}^2 = \sigma_{T_Y}^2 + \sigma_{T_X}^2 - 2\sigma_{T_Y T_X}, \qquad (9.4)$$

and

$$\sigma_{E_D}^2 = \sigma_{E_Y}^2 + \sigma_{E_X}^2. \qquad (9.5)$$

As before, we define the coefficient of reliability for the difference scores, say ρ_D^2, as the ratio of the variance of true difference scores to the variance of observed difference scores.[1] Using Equations 9.4 and 9.5, the reliability coefficient of difference scores D, in terms of the variances of pre- and postmeasures X and Y, their reliability coefficients, and their covariance is

$$\rho_D^2 = \frac{\sigma_{T_D}^2}{\sigma_D^2}$$

$$= \frac{\sigma_{T_Y}^2 + \sigma_{T_X}^2 - 2\sigma_{T_Y T_X}}{\sigma_Y^2 + \sigma_X^2 - 2\sigma_{YX}}$$

$$= \frac{\sigma_Y^2 \rho_Y^2 + \sigma_X^2 \rho_X^2 - 2\sigma_{YX}}{\sigma_Y^2 + \sigma_X^2 - 2\sigma_{YX}}. \qquad (9.6)$$

From the foregoing expression for ρ_D^2, we see that the reliability of difference scores depends on more than the relative amounts of true-score variance in the premeasure X and the postmeasure Y. Another factor affecting ρ_D^2 is the magnitude of the covariance between X and Y. Consider a concrete example: Suppose the coefficients of reliability for X and Y are both 0.9, and their variances are 100 and 120 respectively. If the covariance of X and Y is 0, then the covariance of the true-score variables T_Y and T_X is also 0, and the reliability of the difference score variable D is 0.9. On the other hand, if $\sigma_{XY} = \sigma_{T_Y T_X} = 98.6$, reflecting a correlation between X and Y of 0.9, then ρ_D^2 is only 0.04. Clearly, the observed difference scores will be unreliable indicators of the amount of change that has occurred in individuals when the correlation between scores on the pre- and postmeasures is relatively large. If the correlation ρ_{YX} is reduced from 0.9 to 0.75, while keeping the other parameters constant, then ρ_D^2 is 0.60, a more satisfactory level of reliability.

Another factor to which the coefficient ρ_D^2 is sensitive is change in the variance of the postmeasure, Y. As we have seen, by setting $\sigma_X^2 = 100$, $\sigma_Y^2 = 120$, $\rho_X^2 = \rho_Y^2 = 0.9$, and $\rho_{YX} = 0.75$, we get $\rho_D^2 = 0.6$. If σ_Y^2 now increases, first to 150 and then to 400, with all other factors held constant, the value of ρ_D^2 also increases, first to 0.67, then to 0.75.

Differences in Means and the Issue of Reliability

Having defined the notion of the reliability of difference or change scores, it is now appropriate to draw attention to a potential source of confusion in thinking about the measurement of change: The size of the coefficient of reliability for difference scores reflects neither the size nor the statistical significance of the difference in the means of the distributions of scores on the pre- and postmeasures. The difference in the means of these variables is what we might use, for example, to gauge the effect of a treatment—such as the effect of a diet—on growth in height of children. Imagine for the moment that all children fed a particular diet increase in true height by exactly the same amount between the pre- and postmeasurements, in which case the differences between the pre- and postvalues of true height are exactly the same for all the children. Note that as the situation has been imagined, growth in height is constant even though, as we would expect, the children differ among themselves in the premeasurements and the postmeasurements of height, some being relatively tall and others relatively short. What should be realized for this hypothetical example is the fact that the children cannot be differentiated by the amounts they *gained* in height. Because of this, we should anticipate estimates of zero for both the variance of true-score gains in height and the reliability of the gain (difference) scores.

The issue of the statistical significance of a difference in the means of the pre- and postmeasurements is distinct from, although necessarily related to, the issue of the reliability of the difference measurements. Consider again the example of measuring change in the height of children. The mean gain in height will be judged significantly greater than zero if the mean of the gain scores is more than twice as large as its standard error. (The standard error is equal to the standard deviation of the gain scores divided by the square root of the number of children who were measured.) Statistical significance of this kind is more difficult to realize, obviously, when the variance of the gain scores is large than when it is small. But, as we have seen, the variance of gain scores must be relatively large for gain-score reliability to be relatively large. So, when gain scores are highly reliable, it may be difficult, although by no means impossible, to demonstrate significant gain in the mean. (The larger the sample size, the more likely its mean gain will be judged significant, regardless of the reliability of the gain scores of individuals.)

Fundamental Difficulties in Measuring Change

The treatment of difference scores to this point has ignored two important problems. The first is that the scales of measurement for the pre- and posttests must be identical for the difference score to be interpretable in the units of measurement of either scale. For example, it is possible to interpret gain in height in inches when we use a yardstick graduated in inches to make both the premeasure and postmeasure of height. But how do we interpret a difference in scores on two tests, one used as the premeasure and the other as the postmeasure? This question is not a trivial one for educational and psychological measures because the scaling of two such measures is not obviously the same, even when they are intended to measure the same characteristic. The units of the measuring scales for two tests containing equal numbers of items need not be the same for the reason that the items composing the tests are different—in content, in difficulty and in capacity to discriminate among persons on the characteristic measured by the test. Even using the same test as both premeasure and postmeasure will not necessarily resolve this problem of scale. The experiences of the examinees between the pre- and posttesting may be such as to make it easier to answer some items correctly than others, so the size of the change score for an examinee will depend on whether he or she knew how to answer these items at the time of the pretest. The ideal situation is for the investigator to be in possession of parallel tests of the characteristic, in which case one can be used as the premeasure and the other as the postmeasure.

The second problem we have ignored in the measurement of change is this: For difference scores to be meaningful, the pre- and postmeasures must assess identically the same characteristic. This is a challenging problem for several reasons, including the fact that the changes that occur in a person between the administrations of the premeasure and the postmeasure are likely to involve several different, but related, traits. What is important here is the possibility that, as change occurs in the characteristic of interest, a different trait or configuration of traits comes to control test performance. For example, when administered to young children, a test of addition may demand reasoning, as well as other cognitive processes. When the children are a few months older and certain facts about numbers have been learned and certain arithmetical operations have been practiced to the point of being automatic, the test may involve mostly memory, among other cognitive processes. In this case, the meaning of a change score is unclear. And this lack of clarity will pertain, whether the pre- and postmeasurements are taken by the same test or by parallel tests.

It is too early in the present discussion to advance a conclusion about the measurement of change. Still, the best advice would seem to be that one should avoid trying to measure change. The question being investigated should be recast, so as not to involve change. More about this presently.

Predicting Change

A question sometimes asked is whether it is possible to identify, a priori, the individuals who will change the most during the time between the administrations of the pre- and postmeasures. One predictor we might think of using is the premeasure itself. Unfortunately, this is not a good predictor for the reason that the premeasure and the difference score used to measure change both contain the errors of measurement that are present in the premeasure. But the algebraic sign of these errors of measurement is positive in the premeasure and negative in the change measure, so the covariance and the coefficient of correlation between the premeasure and the change measure are different than they would be were the error term not present in both variables. (The foregoing assertion is substantiated in Sidebar 9.1.)

Consider an example: Suppose the reliability coefficients of a premeasure and a postmeasure are both 0.80, with the variance of the premeasure 225, the variance of the postmeasure 256, and the coefficient of correlation between the pre- and postmeasures 0.65. Then, according to Equation 9.1.4, the covariance of the difference variable D and the premeasure X is equal to (1) the covariance between premeasure and postmeasure, that is, $0.65\sqrt{225}\sqrt{256} = 156$, less (2) the variance of the premeasure, 225, yielding (3) the covariance -69. This result suggests that the persons with the lowest scores on the premeasure are likely to have the largest (positive) change scores. But note the error variance of the premeasure: $\sigma_E^2 = \sigma_X^2(1 - \rho_X^2) = 225(1 - 0.80) = 45$. Without the impact of correlated errors, the estimate of the covariance

Sidebar 9.1

A Demonstration That Correlated Errors of Measurement Can Bias the Prediction of Change

In the following expression, the covariance between observed premeasurements and observed difference measurements are translated into the equivalent expression involving true and error components:

$$\sigma_{XD} = \sigma_{(T_X + E_X), \, [(T_Y - T_X) + (E_Y - E_X)]}$$

$$= \sigma_{T_X, \, (T_Y - T_X)} + \sigma_{E_X, \, (E_Y - E_X)} + \sigma_{E_X, \, (T_Y - T_X)} + \sigma_{T_X, \, (E_Y - E_X)} \, . \tag{9.1.1}$$

The last two terms on the right-hand side of Equation 9.1.1 are zero because, applying classical theory, errors are presumed to be independent of true scores. As for the first two terms on the right-hand side of Equation 9.1.1,

$$\sigma_{T_X, \, (T_Y - T_X)} = \sigma_{T_X T_Y} - \sigma_{T_X}^2$$

$$= \sigma_{XY} - \sigma_{T_X}^2 \, , \tag{9.1.2}$$

and

$$\sigma_{E_X, \, (E_Y - E_X)} = \sigma_{E_X E_Y} - \sigma_{E_X}^2$$

$$= -\sigma_{E_X}^2 \, , \tag{9.1.3}$$

the simplification of the right-hand side of Equation 9.1.3 follows from the fact that the error random variables of two independent measures are uncorrelated. Thus we have

$$\sigma_{XD} = \sigma_{XY} - \sigma_{T_X}^2 - \sigma_{E_X}^2$$

$$= \sigma_{XY} - \sigma_X^2 \, . \tag{9.1.4}$$

This covariance is different from what it would be were the errors of measurement in the premeasure X not also present, with opposite algebraic sign, in the measure of change, D. Consequently, the coefficient of correlation between the premeasure and the simple difference measure of change is different from what it would be without the effect of correlated errors. In fact, in unusual circumstances, the two correlation coefficients, one with and one without the correlated error term, might even have opposite algebraic signs.

between the difference variable D and the premeasure X is only -24—
still negative, but much weaker than the covariance that includes the
negative bias due to correlated errors of measurement.

If an unbiased indicator of the relationship between premeasure and
change is desired, the investigator can obtain it as follows: At the time
the premeasure is taken, he or she should measure the characteristic
twice, using parallel tests. Then one of the premeasures can be used to
calculate the difference scores and the other can be used as the covariate
of the difference scores. The error variance term in Equation 9.1.4 now
disappears because the errors of measurement on the parallel premeasures are independent.

Studying Profiles

It is frequently the case in academic and employment counseling that an
individual will be administered a battery of tests. An examinee's performance on the different tests in the battery might then be portrayed graphi-
cally, with the examinee's scores plotted in the fashion depicted in Figure
9.1. The purpose of such a *profile* graph or *profile* chart is to facilitate a
comparison of the examinee's performances on the different tests, and also
to facilitate a comparison of the examinee's profile with that of a reference
group (e.g., professional engineers or doctors who practice family medi-
cine), the latter profile being constructed from the means of the scores
achieved on the tests by a sample of the reference group.

One might wonder how it is possible to compare an examinee's
performance on a test of spatial ability with his or her scores on tests of
spelling, mathematical computation, and so on. Such comparisons as
these would seem to pose a challenge not unlike the proverbial challenge of comparing apples and oranges. But just as it is possible to
compare apples and oranges on such characteristics as color, sweetness,
and vitamin C content, so it is possible to compare a person's *relative
standing* in a reference group on tests of different mental characteristics,
for example, tests of verbal, mathematical, and spatial abilities. What
we require is that the score scales of the different tests be comparable
in some sense. Achieving scale comparability might seem to be a
daunting task. In practice, the tests in a battery are administered to a
well-defined group of examinees, and the distribution of scores for each
test is converted into the standard-score metric or one derived from the
standard-score metric. (In addition, the standard scores might be based
on a transformed distribution of raw scores, with the transformation

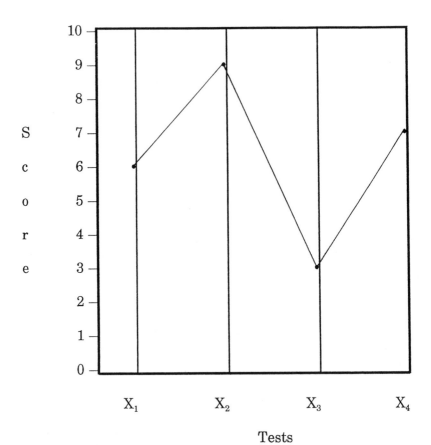

Figure 9.1. A Profile Graph or Profile Chart of an Examinee's Scores on the Four Tests in a Hypothetical Battery of Tests

being designed, for example, to make the distribution as nearly normal as possible.) It is an examinee's standard scores on the different tests that are then compared. (For further details, see Angoff, 1971.)

The SEM for Difference Scores

One might wonder how an examinee's scores on two or more tests can be compared, other than by eye, in the profile chart. The discussion of the reliability of difference scores is relevant here. Although we are no longer considering differences between pre- and postmeasures of the same characteristic, we are nevertheless considering the relative importance of differences among the standard scores an examinee achieves on the tests in a battery. The difference between any pair of standard scores for the examinee should be judged against the standard error of measurement for the difference between two scores. The null hypothesis that is put up for rejection is that the examinee's true standard scores on the two tests are identical; in other words, that their difference is 0. Given this null hypothesis, Equation 9.5 gives the standard error of the difference between an examinee's observed standard scores on the two tests. Assuming the variance of errors of measurement on the two tests are identical, the standard error of measurement of the difference between an examinee's test scores is $\sigma_{E_D} = \sqrt{2}\sigma_{E_X}$, where σ_{E_X} is the standard error of measurement of either of the two tests.

To see the foregoing ideas in application, suppose a person has standard scores of 1.5 and 1.8 on a verbal test and a spatial test, respectively. If the reliability of each test is 0.9, the standard error of measurement (in the standard-score metric) of each test is $\sigma_X\sqrt{1 - \rho_X^2} = 1\sqrt{1 - 0.9} = \sqrt{0.1} = 0.32$. (Note that $\sigma_X = 1$ because we are dealing with standard scores.) Inasmuch as the difference of 0.3 ($= 1.5 - 1.8$) in the examinee's standard scores on the two tests is less than the SEM of the difference, which SEM is 0.45 [$= \sqrt{2}(0.32)$], we conclude that the examinee's standings on the two tests are not significantly different.

Other Difference Scores

In addition to the simple difference score, several other measures of change have been proposed. One of these, suggested by F. M. Lord (1956, 1958, 1963), is estimated true change, with the pre- and postmeasures being used to obtain a linear-regression estimate of the difference between true scores on the two tests. Cronbach and Furby (1970) noted that concomitant measures, in addition to the pre- and postmeasures, could be used to improve estimates of true change.

Another measure is the residual-change score, discussed by Manning and DuBois (1962). Linear regression is used to predict scores on the postmeasure from observed scores on the premeasure. The observed residual measure of change is the difference for a person between observed and predicted scores on the postmeasure. A conceptually related measure is true residual change, proposed by Tucker, Damarin, and Messick (1966): True scores on the pre- and postmeasures are used to define a score consisting of that part of the true score on the postmeasure that cannot be predicted from the true score on the premeasure. These different measures of change possess associated formulas for reliability coefficients, all different in some way from Equation 9.6 for the reliability of simple difference scores. But neither of these coefficients is considered further, for reasons made clear in the following section.

Why Bother With Change in Social Science Research?

It would be appropriate to consider the foregoing measures of change in more detail, perhaps even suggesting circumstances in which one or the other might be preferred, were it not for the discouraging remarks that must be offered in response to the two questions usually asked in studies of change—(1) How much has been gained as a consequence of some treatment? (2) Is it possible to predict before the event which persons will change the most? As noted earlier, a besetting difficulty arises when the attempt is made to answer these questions, a difficulty associated with the scaling of educational and psychological variables. In tracking growth in the height of children using a yardstick, there is no question that the scale of measurement for the premeasure is the same as the scale of measurement for the postmeasure. The yardstick used on one occasion is for all practical purposes identical to that used on another occasion, even when physically it is a different stick. Also reassuring is the perceptually obvious fact that the units on a yardstick are the same, whether they occur near one end, the middle, or the other end of the stick. The same cannot be said about educational and psychological measures. So-called parallel tests are never perfectly that, so the characteristic measured by one test is almost certainly somewhat different from that measured by its putative parallel version, and this difference is exacerbated by any real change in the nature of the attributes being measured between the administration of the pre- and postmeasures. Moreover, the units of the educational or psychological test are almost certainly not constant all along the scale, from low scores through middle to high scores. This means that change near the low end of the scale is not necessarily comparable with change near the middle or the high end of the scale, even though the numerical index of change, say the simple difference between observed scores, might be the same for individuals at all three locations.

The advice of Cronbach and Furby (1970), which is endorsed here, is to frame questions about change in educational and psychological variables in other ways. For example, the investigator who asks about growth in a characteristic due to some educational treatment might instead be encouraged to ask about the difference in mean postmeasure scores achieved by an experimental group and a control group, with scores on the premeasure used either as a covariate or as a blocking variable in assigning individuals to the treatment groups. And instead of asking which students gained the most in the time between the administration of the pre- and postmeasures, an investigator might try to determine how well true scores on the postmeasure can be predicted from true scores on the premeasure. Neither of these approaches requires the calculation of difference scores.

A Different Perspective on the Measurement of Change

It should not be thought that the advice offered in the preceding section represents the last word on the subject of change measurement. A very different perspective is offered by Rogosa, Brandt, and Zimowski (1982), Rogosa, Floden, and Willett (1984), and Rogosa and Willett (1983, 1985), a perspective that has been advanced in a persuasive and readable review essay by Willett (1988-1989). These authors adopt what Willett called the "*longitudinal* approach" (p. 347, italics in the original), in which "multiple waves of data are collected on a sample of individuals over time, and an explicit model of individual growth is adopted as the basis for the statistical analysis" (p. 347). The idea is to measure some characteristic of a person at regular intervals, so that eventually three or more measurements of the characteristic are available for each person being studied. The growth or change in the characteristic over the repeated measurements is modeled separately for each person, possibly as a straight line relating the measurements to the time or occasion of measurement. Differences among persons in the parameters of the model—the slope and intercept of the straight line, for example—are the outcomes that would be used by those interested in studying how the characteristic changes over time.

The approach advanced by Rogosa, Willett, and others depends critically on the assumption that the tests used to follow change through time do in fact measure the same characteristic. Moreover, the tests must provide measurements that are on the same scale, with the units of measurement being constant all along the scale. Willett (1988-1989) stated these assumptions as follows: "that the outcomes being investigated are measured by instruments that maintain their construct validity over time and that the obtained scores remain equatable from occasion to occasion" (p. 352). These assumptions should not be accepted without question for measures of most attributes of interest to social science researchers. Nevertheless, if the assumptions can be accepted and this approach is adopted, the matter of reliability will arise in connection with the parameters of the growth model—the slope of the line, for example—used to characterize change (see Willett, 1988-1989, pp. 402-406).

Reliability Theory for Criterion-Referenced Measurements

Thus far our view of measurement has been substantially that which we form as children, from our experience of measuring length and weight. It is obvious, perceptually, that buildings differ in height and persons differ in size. The purpose of measurement is to ascertain the heights of buildings or the weights of individuals, and in the process produce results that correspond to perceived reality. Differences in height or weight can then be noted and used for whatever purpose they were obtained to serve. There is no thought in this naive view that measuring scales have been or even could be constructed so as to exaggerate differences in building height or body weight. That differences exist is obvious. Measurement serves only to describe the differences in a standard way, so that they may be readily understood by all persons familiar with the measuring scale.

Mental measurement is a very different enterprise from that of measuring height and weight. Differences among persons with respect to a kind of educational achievement or to a psychological characteristic are not palpable. Even though some sense of individual differences can perhaps be inferred from differences in the answers various students give in school classes or from differences in the way they perform the common tasks of everyday life, there exist no universally accepted and obviously valid yardsticks for describing these differences in standard numerical terms. This being the case, developers of educational and psychological measures have had to invent ways of ascribing meaning to such seemingly arbitrary measurements as the number of correct answers to the items in a test. Either of two approaches has been taken. In one, a person's performance on a test is interpreted in relation to the performance of a representative sample of some well-defined population. This is the so-called *norm-referenced approach* to measurement. Alternatively, an attempt is made to refer test scores to more or less absolute standards of performance that derive from or reflect the content and nature of the tasks performed. This is the *criterion-referenced approach*. These two approaches to measurement seem to require different conceptions of reliability, which are spelled out in more detail in the following two sections.

Reliability in the Context of Norm-Referenced Measurement

Norm-referenced tests produce measurements that are interpretable in terms of where they occur in the distribution of scores for some well-defined group. The driving concepts of norm-referenced testing are those of individual differences and test-score variance. A test question answered in the same way by everyone for whom the test is intended—all correct or all incorrect—serves no useful purpose in norm-referenced testing because such a question fails to discriminate among the persons tested. For example, a good test of vocabulary, according to norm-referenced philosophy, should contain words that some persons know and that other persons do not. Moreover, the scores associated with the responses to any one of the questions selected for the vocabulary test should be positively correlated with the scores associated with the responses to any of the other questions. When the scores for every pair of items in a test are positively correlated, the total scores on the test will spread widely across the score scale of the test. So we expect the observed-score variance for a norm-referenced test to be relatively large. When observed-score variance is relatively large, it is possible also for true-score variance to be relatively large, in which case the reliability of the test scores—reliability in the sense in which we have been considering it—will be relatively high.

Some writers have suggested that norm-referenced item selection of the sort described in the preceding paragraph is implied by classical reliability theory (see, e.g., Popham & Husek, 1969). We can discern nothing in classical theory that would support this suggestion. It is one thing to note that a norm-referenced approach to item selection will produce reliable test scores, if reliable scores are possible, and quite another to suggest that classical reliability theory is based on a norm-referenced approach to test development. Classical reliability theory gives meaning to the notion of reliability in terms of observed-, true-, and error-score variance, and these notions apply whether or not a norm-referenced approach to test development and score interpretation is adopted.

Criterion-Referenced Measurement

The issue for this kind of measurement is one of defining clearly what the test measures, either by carefully describing the domain of content assessed by the test or by explicitly delineating the theoretical construct that is to be measured. Performance on a test is then reported with reference to the domain description or delineated construct, not with reference to how other persons performed on the test. A criterion-referenced test should result in a description of test performance that conveys information as to what the person knows or can do in terms that are independent of the way anyone else performs on the test.

A possible example of a criterion-referenced test report is the statement that an individual's test performance indicates he or she can perform the arithmetic operations of addition, subtraction, multiplication, and division on two-digit numbers. This report carries meaning that seems both interpretable and independent of anyone else's performance on the test.

Beyond the issue of direct interpretability, the issue of variance needs to be considered in the context of criterion-referenced measurement. Variance in item responses is not an irrelevant consideration, even for the developer of a criterion-referenced test, for the obvious reason that the constructor of such a test wants to distinguish examinees who have the skill and knowledge required to answer a question correctly from examinees who do not. But the lack of variance is not necessarily bad from the perspective of the criterion-referenced tester. For example, if it should happen that all examinees correctly answer all the questions on a criterion-referenced test, then, *provided the test represents the attribute or behavior domain adequately,* it will have served to indicate that these individuals all possess similar knowledge or ability in relation to the attribute or domain tested, and so should all receive the same reports of test performance.

Decision Consistency as Reliability

Inasmuch as a criterion-referenced test will not necessarily yield a set of highly variable test scores, the coefficient of reliability, ρ_X^2, will not necessarily provide useful information about the quality of scores on a criterion-referenced test. What is needed is a conception of consistency that might result in a high coefficient, even when all examinees perform on the test in exactly the same way, or very nearly so. The notion of decision consistency suggests a kind of reliability that seems appropriate for at least some criterion-referenced testing situations. In particular, it seems appropriate for describing the degree of consistency that is realized when educational and psychological measures are used to make pass/fail decisions about examinees (Traub & Rowley, 1980).

To elaborate: In certain testing situations a judgment is made about whether or not a student's test performance is satisfactory, about whether or not the test score is high enough to be regarded as passing. This kind of judgment can be made independently of the performance of other persons, and although the information that a test score is satisfactory or passing tells us nothing about the domain of content or the construct measured by the test, it does convey a direct impression of quality of performance. In this limited sense, then, testing for the purpose of making pass/fail judgments can be said to be criterion-referenced. Persons whose scores exceed the cutting point on the score scale of the test are sometimes referred to as "masters," those whose scores do not, as "non-masters." Masters are those deemed to have succeeded, at least to the point that their test performance is satisfactory; they may be passed to the next unit of work, awarded a certificate of accomplishment, and so forth. Non-masters are deemed not to have succeeded to the desired extent and are failed in some sense that might include requiring a unit of work to be repeated, denying the award of a certificate, and the like. In this context, the desirable test is one that, in a repeated measurement study, would produce scores leading to the same pass/fail decisions each time it or a parallel form were administered.[2] This is the notion of decision consistency, which underlies one conception of reliability for criterion-referenced tests. The idea of decision consistency was advanced by Hambleton and Novick (1973) and made operational by Swaminathan, Hambleton, and Algina (1974).

The Coefficient of Decision Consistency

Decision consistency can be indexed relatively easily in the situation where there are only two mastery states, and a test is administered twice or retesting is done with a parallel form. Consider the fourfold table in Figure 9.2. The cells of the table give the numbers of persons observed for each possible combination of pass and fail decisions based on replicate test scores. The cells corresponding to pass/pass and fail/fail represent decisions that are the same for both tests. The other two cells represent the combinations of scores for which the decision was different for the two test scores—fail/pass or pass/fail. A simple index of decision consistency, say π_{dc}, can be defined as the proportion of examinees for which the decisions are the same for both tests. Given the frequencies defined in Figure 9.2, a sample estimate of π_{dc} would be

$$\hat{\pi}_{dc} = \frac{N_{pp}}{N_{++}} + \frac{N_{ff}}{N_{++}}$$

$$= \frac{N_{pp} + N_{ff}}{N_{++}}. \tag{9.7}$$

The larger π_{dc}, or its sample estimate, $\hat{\pi}_{dc}$, the greater the consistency with which examinees are assigned to the passing and failing groups on the two test administrations. Moreover, the index π_{dc} has an important advantage over the reliability coefficient ρ_X^2 : When all examinees in a population pass the first administration of a test and all also pass either a re-administration of the same test or the administration of a parallel form, the index π_{dc} attains the maximum possible value of 1. In other words, there is no need for a test to discriminate among examinees in the sense that some are passed and others are failed in order for π_{dc} to be relatively large.

The computation of $\hat{\pi}_{dc}$ can be illustrated using the data reported in Table 9.1. The values $N_{pp} = 75$, $N_{ff} = 5$, and $N_{++} = 100$, when substituted in Equation 9.7, give $\hat{\pi}_{dc} = 0.80$. Note that for this index to describe the decision consistency of the test, the examinees who are tested twice should not have changed on the characteristic being measured between testing occasions. The tests should be administered relatively close together in time, and not, for example, as pre- and posttests for an instructional unit.

Correcting π_{dc} for Agreement Due to Chance

One criticism of π_{dc} is that it will be greater than zero even when the observed scores on a test are totally unreliable in the sense of classical reliability theory. To see this, suppose that the pass/fail cutting score, X_c, falls in the middle of a distribution of scores, with half the examinees achieving scores of X_c or more (passing) and half achieving scores of less than X_c (failing). If the test is totally unreliable, the probability that a person will obtain a score of X_c or more is 0.5, the proportion of

First Test		Second Test		Row Sums
		Fail	Pass	
Pass		N_{pf}	N_{pp}	N_{p+}
Fail		N_{ff}	N_{fp}	N_{f+}
Column Sums		N_{+f}	N_{+p}	N_{++}

Figure 9.2. A cross-classification of examinees by performance on two administrations of the same test or on separate administrations of two parallel tests, the administrations occurring in close temporal proximity. The cells of the table contain the numbers of examinees passing both tests, passing one and failing the other, or failing both. The marginal frequencies give the sums of the cell counts by rows and columns. When most examinees are classified pass/pass or fail/fail (i.e., when $N_{pp} + N_{ff}$ is nearly equal to N_{++}), decision consistency is high.

the examinees achieving a passing score. The expectation, then, is that one half the persons who passed a test on its first administration will also pass either a re-administration of the same test or the administration of a parallel form, and one half will fail. Also, one half of the persons who failed the first administration of the test can be expected to fail on retaking it or on taking instead a parallel form, but half can be expected to pass. In other words, π_{dc} will be 0.5 for this situation, even though it is simply a matter of chance whether or not a person scores above the cutting score.

To correct the problem described in the preceding paragraph, Swaminathan et al. (1974) suggested the use of Coefficient kappa, symbolized here as κ_{dc}. Using the quantities symbolized in Figure 9.2, Coefficient kappa is defined as follows:

$$\kappa_{dc} = \frac{\pi_{dc} - \pi_c}{1 - \pi_c}, \qquad (9.8)$$

where

TABLE 9.1 Example Fourfold Table for Calculating Indices of Decision
Consistency

		Second Test		Row Sums
		Fail	Pass	
First Test	Pass	5	75	80
	Fail	5	15	20
Column Sums		10	90	100

$$\hat{\pi}_{dc} = \frac{75+5}{100} = 0.80$$

$$\hat{\pi}_{c} = \left(\frac{80}{100}\right)\left(\frac{90}{100}\right) + \left(\frac{10}{100}\right)\left(\frac{20}{100}\right) = 0.72 + 0.02 = 0.74$$

$$\hat{\kappa}_{dc} = \frac{0.80 - 0.74}{1.00 - 0.74} = 0.23$$

$$\hat{\pi}_{c} = \left(\frac{N_{+p}}{N_{++}}\right)\left(\frac{N_{p+}}{N_{++}}\right) + \left(\frac{N_{+f}}{N_{++}}\right)\left(\frac{N_{f+}}{N_{++}}\right)$$

$$= \frac{N_{+p}N_{p+}}{N_{++}^2} + \frac{N_{+f}N_{f+}}{N_{++}^2}$$

is the proportion of persons who are expected by chance either to pass both
test administrations or fail both test administrations. This expected number
is calculated on the assumptions (1) that an examinee's performance on the
first test is independent, in the sense described in Chapter 6, of his
performance on the second test, and (2) that the marginal frequencies of
Figure 9.2, namely N_{+p}, N_{p+}, N_{+f} and N_{f+}, are fixed.

A sense of the difference between π_{dc} and κ_{dc} can be derived from the example of Table 9.1. Given the frequencies in this table, the estimate of the decision consistency index, $\hat{\pi}_{dc}$, is, as noted before, 0.80. But the estimate of the corrected index, $\hat{\kappa}_{dc}$, is only 0.23, reflecting the fact that, given the marginal frequencies in Table 9.1, a relatively high level of agreement in the pass and fail decisions made on the basis of the results of the two test administrations can be expected to occur by chance.

Suppose we were free to manipulate the cell frequencies of such a table as Table 9.1, all the while keeping the marginal frequencies fixed. How large could the values of $\hat{\pi}_{dc}$ and $\hat{\kappa}_{dc}$ become? It turns out that the maximum possible value of $\hat{\kappa}_{dc}$, say $\kappa_{dc_{MAX}}$, for the marginal frequencies given in Table 9.1 is 0.62. This maximum would occur if the coefficient of decision consistency, $\hat{\pi}_{dc}$, were also as large as it could be, given the marginal frequencies. For Table 9.1, the maximum value of $\hat{\pi}_{dc}$ is 0.90. This value would occur if all the persons who passed the first test also passed the second, in which case N_{pp} would be 80. To maintain the marginal frequencies, N_{ff} would have to be 10; N_{pf}, 0; and N_{fp}, 10. Because the marginal frequencies have been held constant, the value of $\hat{\pi}_c$ is also constant at 0.74. Substituting these results in Equation 9.8, we find $\hat{\kappa}_{dc_{MAX}}$ is 0.62.

The foregoing example illustrates a problem that arises whenever the marginal frequency distributions are not the same for both dimensions of a two-by-two table, and the frequencies are presumed to be fixed. Then the cell frequencies of the table are constrained such that it is impossible for every observation to fall into either of just two cells, pass/pass and fail/fail. On the other hand, if the marginal frequency distributions of the two-by-two table are the same for both tests, and no observations fall in the pass/fail and fail/pass cells, then $\hat{\pi}_{dc} = \hat{\kappa}_{dc} = 1$.

There lies in the preceding paragraph the suggestion of another consistency index: $\hat{\kappa}_{dc}/\hat{\kappa}_{dc_{MAX}}$. This ratio would have a maximum value of 1.00, as does the coefficient of decision consistency π_{dc}.

Which Index to Use?

Given that three indices of decision consistency have been proposed, which of them should be used and when? Unfortunately, clear-cut answers do not exist for these questions. Each index provides a different perspective on decision consistency. Moreover, as noted by Traub and Rowley (1980) with reference to π_{dc} and κ_{dc}:

The relationship between $[\pi_{dc}]$ and $[\kappa_{dc}]$ is not a simple one. It depends on the shapes of the distributions of scores on Test 1 and Test 2, whether they are unimodal and symmetric or not; on the magnitude of the correlation between scores on the two tests; and on the location of the cutting score X_c [on the test score scale]. (p. 530)

In view of the computational simplicity of π_{dc} and κ_{dc}, we suggest that both be computed, as was recommended by Millman (1979). In addition, $\hat{\kappa}_{dc}/\hat{\kappa}_{dc_{MAX}}$ could be computed very easily. All three indices are relatively easy to interpret, although π_{dc} is most straightforward in this regard.

Single-Administration Estimates of Decision Consistency

In most mastery testing situations, it is not feasible to impose a second test administration on examinees. For example, in certification testing, where examinees are attempting to gain a certificate of competence or a license to practice a profession, motivation would be high to perform well on the first test. But anyone who passed this test would not be motivated to take a second test seriously, unless it too were required as part of the certification process. Double jeopardy is unpalatable, so examinees are almost never asked to pass a test twice in order to be certified. Experiments that generate two-way classifications of the kind illustrated in Figure 9.1 are rarely, if ever, conducted. Instead, theory is invoked to produce an estimate of π_{dc}.

Subkoviak Index of Decision Consistency. The method to be described was proposed by Subkoviak (1976). This method rests on statistical theory for binomial variables. It is assumed that the test under consideration consists only of items that elicit dichotomously scorable responses. Suppose there are n such items, and that they have been sampled from a large population of items. Suppose, too, that person p can respond correctly to a proportion ζ_p of the items in the population of items, and so will get scores of 1 on this fraction of the items. (ζ, by the way, is the Greek letter zeta.) Responses to the other items in the population will be incorrect, and so will be scored 0. Thus the entity ζ_p is the proportion-correct true score for person p. Given the foregoing framework, person p's responses to n items drawn at random from the population of items can be viewed as n trials of a binomial process. The probability is ζ_p that the response to an item will be scored 1, and the probability is $1 - \zeta_p$ that the response will, instead, be scored 0. For example, if ζ_p were 0.7 and the person responded to 100 items, we would expect him or her to answer 70 correctly, and so earn a test score, X_p, of 70.

Suppose that X_p must be at least X_c $(0 < X_c \leq n)$ for person p to pass the test. We may ask what the probability is that person p will score 1 on each of at least X_c of n items, given that he or she could achieve a score of 1 for his or her answers to $100 \cdot \zeta_p\%$ of the items in the universe of all possible items. The binomial probability that person p will correctly answer exactly X_c of n items drawn at random from the universe of items is

$$\pi_{p, X_c} = \binom{n}{X_c} (\zeta_p)^{X_c} (1 - \zeta_p)^{(n - X_c)}, \tag{9.9}$$

where $\binom{n}{X_c}$ is the number of different ways of choosing X_c of the n items to be answered correctly. Note that $\binom{n}{X_c} = \frac{n!}{X_c!(n - X_c)!}$, with $n! = n \cdot (n - 1) \cdot (n - 2) \cdots 2 \cdot 1$ and $0! = 1$. So, for example, if $n = 10$ and $X_c = 7$, then

$$\binom{10}{7} = \frac{10!}{7!(10 - 7)!} = \frac{10 \cdot 9 \cdot 8 \cdot 7 \cdot 6 \cdot 5 \cdot 4 \cdot 3 \cdot 2 \cdot 1}{7 \cdot 6 \cdot 5 \cdot 4 \cdot 3 \cdot 2 \cdot 1 \cdot 3 \cdot 2 \cdot 1} = \frac{10 \cdot 9 \cdot 8}{3 \cdot 2 \cdot 1} = 120.$$

The person will also pass if he or she obtains a score of 1 on each of $X_c + 1$ items, $X_c + 2$ items, . . . , $(n - 1)$ items, or all n items. The probability of each of these events is defined using a modified version of Equation 9.9, substituting $X_c + 1$, $X_c + 2$, . . . , $(n - 1)$ and n in turn for X_c. Thus the binomial probability that person p will pass an n-item test by obtaining a score of 1 on at least X_c items is given by

$$\pi_p = \sum_{j = X_c}^{n} \pi_{p, j}$$

$$= \sum_{j = X_c}^{n} \binom{n}{j} (\zeta_p)^j (1 - \zeta_p)^{n - j}. \tag{9.10}$$

Complementing π_p is the probability $(1 - \pi_p)$ that person p will not pass the n-item test, that is, will correctly answer fewer than X_c of the items in the test.

Next, suppose that a second sample of n items were randomly drawn from the universe of items and administered to person p. The probability that the person would get at least X_c items correct on this test, assuming no change in ζ_p, is that given by Equation 9.10, and the probability of not responding correctly to as many as X_c of the items on the second test would again be $1 - \pi_p$. Provided the items on the two tests are independent random samples of the items in the population of items, the probability that person p is classified consistently as passing or failing on both tests is given by

$$S_{dc_p} = (\pi_p)^2 + (1 - \pi_p)^2 , \qquad (9.11)$$

where S_{dc_p} stands for "Subkoviak coefficient of decision consistency for person p." Over the N persons in a sample of persons, the Subkoviak coefficient of decision consistency is defined to be

$$S_{dc} = \frac{\sum_{p=1}^{N} [(\pi_p)^2 + (1 - \pi_p)^2]}{N} . \qquad (9.12)$$

A demonstration of the calculation of S_{dc} for a set of test scores can be found in Sidebar 9.2.

The derivation of Equation 9.12 rests on the assumed independence, for person p, of scores on the test actually taken and the hypothetical second test (given the fixed true ability ζ_p of person p). It also rests on the assumed validity of the binomial process as a representation of the response process of the test taker. Subkoviak (1976) commented on these matters as follows:

> The independence assumption does not seem overly restrictive, since it amounts to the supposition that errors of measurement on parallel tests are independent for each person [p]. This would tend to be the case if the tests contain different items and are administered at different times, and these are the conditions for which one generally estimates reliability.
>
> The binomial assumption, on the other hand, is an oversimplification of reality with regard to the condition that outcomes on items be independent and with regard to the condition that the probability of a correct response remain constant across items. Nonetheless, the simple binomial model [of Equation 9.10] is flexible enough to approximate the different forms of [score] distributions that result as individual abilities vary from near the "floor" of a test, through the midrange, and to the "ceiling." (p. 268)

Sidebar 9.2

A DEMONSTRATION OF THE APPLICATION OF SUBKOVIAK'S APPROACH TO
ESTIMATING DECISION CONSISTENCY

We assume the availability of observed scores for 10 examinees on a test composed of ten dichotomously scored items. (To conform with the assumptions of binomial theory, the 10 items should be a random sample from a large population of items. Moreover, each person tested should be given a different random sample of 10 items. In most practical situations, however, there exists only one test, which is given to all examinees. For this reason, the resulting coefficient approximates the one that was theoretically justified in the derivation of Equation 9.12.) Further, it is assumed that to pass the test an examinee must achieve a score of 7 or more. The binomial probabilities of achieving a score of 7 or more correct answers, given a true score equal to the fraction obtained by dividing an examinee's observed score by 10, is given in the column of the table headed $P(X) \geq 7$. The probability of NOT achieving a score of at least 7 is given in the column headed $P(X) < 7$. These results lead, for each examinee, to the probability of passing both of two tests, given the examinee's estimated proportion correct true score, $\hat{\zeta}_p$; this probability is given in the column of the table headed $[P(X) \geq 7]^2$. The probability of failing both of two tests is given in the column headed $[P(X) < 7]^2$. When these two probabilities are combined, using Equation 9.11, we obtain an estimate of the probability of a consistent decision about the examinee (pass/pass or fail/fail) from the administration of two tests. The latter probability is given in the last column of the table. When the sum of these probabilities, 8.04, is divided by 10, the number of examinees, we have the Subkoviak index of decision consistency, in this case 0.80.

Person	X_p	$\hat{\zeta}_p$	$P(X) \geq 7$	$P(X) < 7$	$[P(X) \geq 7]^2$	$[P(X) < 7]^2$	$[P(X) \geq 7]^2 +$ $[P(X) < 7]^2$
1	5	0.5	0.17	0.83	0.03	0.69	0.72
2	2	0.2	0.00	1.00	0.00	1.00	1.00
3	4	0.4	0.05	0.95	0.00	0.89	0.90
4	9	0.9	0.99	0.01	0.97	0.00	0.97
5	6	0.6	0.38	0.62	0.15	0.38	0.53
6	4	0.4	0.05	0.95	0.00	0.89	0.90
7	3	0.3	0.01	0.99	0.00	0.98	0.98
8	6	0.6	0.38	0.62	0.15	0.38	0.53
9	9	0.9	0.99	0.01	0.97	0.00	0.97
10	7	0.7	0.66	0.35	0.42	0.12	0.54
						Sum	8.04

NOTE: The entries in the table have been rounded to two decimal places, so some of the squared terms may not appear to be correct.

Estimating ζ_p. To implement Subkoviak's procedure, we need an estimate of each examinee's proportion-correct true score, ζ_p. A reasonable estimator is the quantity $\hat{\zeta}_p = X_p/n$, where X_p is the number of the n items for which person p's responses produced scores of 1. This is the so-called maximum likelihood estimator of ζ_p. The standard error of this statistic, $\sqrt{\zeta_p(1 - \zeta_p)/n}$, will be small for reasonably long tests. A small standard error is desirable because then we can expect the estimate to be reasonably close to the true value ζ_p. (This expectation also requires that the estimate of ζ_p not be biased.) Subkoviak suggested that n should be larger than 40.

Other Estimators of ζ_p. Among the estimators of ζ_p, other than X_p/n, that have been suggested is the linear regression estimate. Consider for the moment the true score $\tau_p = n\cdot\zeta_p$. The linear regression estimate of τ_p is obtained from the observed score X_p as follows:

$$R(\hat{\tau}_p) = \rho_X^2 \cdot X_p + (1 - \rho_X^2) \cdot \overline{X}, \qquad (9.13)$$

where $\overline{X}$ is the mean score of the N persons in the sample of persons. [Dividing $R(\hat{\tau}_p)$ by n will convert it into a regression estimate of ζ_p. We do not indicate how the reliability coefficient ρ_X^2 is or should be estimated; aside from the fact that it must be a number between 0 and 1, the precise nature of ρ_X^2 is otherwise irrelevant to the present discussion.] The effect of taking group membership into account is to estimate the person's true score to be a number nearer the mean score of the group than is the observed score. The smaller the coefficient of reliability ρ_X^2, the nearer the regression estimate of true score will be to the group mean. When the reliability coefficient is large, greater weight is placed on the observed score than on the group mean in estimating the true score, as seems appropriate.

A problem with regression estimates of true scores is their dependence on the group mean and the reliability coefficient, both of which are characteristics of the group. Everyone is a member of many different groups. If the reference group is changed, the regression estimate of true score is also changed. This may seem reasonable, but it creates an awkward situation in dealing with the score of an individual; which is the true score that should be used to characterize him or her?

A technical problem with regression estimates of true scores is that they are biased, which is to say their expected value, over trials of the repeated measurement experiment, is not the true score τ_p, which is the mean of the observed score random variable X for person p. The observed score X_p, on the other hand, is an unbiased estimate of τ_p, which is to say $\varepsilon X_p = \tau_p$.

Some empirical research has been addressed to the matter of which of the different estimators of ζ_p is to be preferred (Algina & Noe, 1978; Spray & Welch, 1990; Subkoviak, 1978). This research suggests that in practical work involving tests of reasonable length, say 40 items or more, the maximum likelihood estimator of ζ_p, namely the observed proportion correct, can be expected to produce acceptable results.

Huynh's Estimate of Decision Consistency. Subkoviak's is not the only single-administration estimator of decision consistency that has been proposed. Another index was suggested by Huynh (1976). Huynh's approach is based on more complex theory than Subkoviak's, and is beyond the scope of the present treatment of the topic. It is not clear that Huynh's index offers any important advantages in practical work with tests that are reasonably long.

Other Approaches to Estimating the Reliability of Criterion-Referenced Tests

Approaches different from the decision-consistency index have been proposed for describing the consistency of decisions based on criterion-referenced measurements. These are beyond the scope of this treatment; for a review, see Traub and Rowley (1980).

Summary

In this chapter we have considered several reliability-related issues that arise in two special contexts—measuring change and criterion-referenced measurement. With regard to the first of these, one particular measure of change, the simple difference score, was considered in detail. An expression for the coefficient of reliability for simple difference scores was derived and shown to be sensitive to the degree of correlation between the pre- and postmeasurements used in calculating difference scores. Also, the reliability coefficients and the variances of the pre- and postmeasures were shown to affect the reliability coefficient of simple difference scores. Several other approaches to the measurement of change were considered, but not in detail. The reasons for giving change such short shrift are (i) the scales of the measuring instruments used in social science research are unlikely to involve units of measurement that are constant across the scale, (ii) the characteristics measured by a test may change during the time between pre- and posttesting, and (iii) very often social science research questions that seem to involve the concept of change can be addressed in ways not requiring this concept.

As for reliability in the context of criterion-referenced measurement, it was noted that this kind of measurement, which by definition involves scores directly interpretable in terms of what a person knows or can do, and not in terms of how others perform on the test, is sometimes associated with pass/fail decision making. Reliability in this context can be conceptualized as consistency in the making of pass and fail decisions. Three indices related to the consistency of pass/fail decisions were defined, these for the situation in which independent decisions of pass and fail are made on the basis of two independent test administrations. These indices are the proportion of consistent decisions (π_{dc}), the proportion of consistent decisions corrected for the effects of chance (κ_{dc}), and the ratio of κ_{dc} to the maximum possible proportion of consistent decisions corrected for the effects of chance ($\kappa_{dc}/\kappa_{dc_{MAX}}$). It was recommended that, when decision consistency is the reliability concept of choice, all three coefficients be calculated; the effort required is small and each offers a different perspective on decision consistency. In the likely event that only one test is administered, Subkoviak's (1976) approach to estimating decision consistency was described and illustrated.

Exercises

9.1. A course has been designed to improve the ability of college students to do algebra. An investigator hypothesized that the abilities of students who initially score low on an algebra test will improve more after having taken the course than will the abilities of students who initially score high on the test. An experiment was then conducted to test the foregoing hypothesis. In the experiment, two parallel tests were developed, with one of these tests used to obtain an initial measure (premeasure) of algebra ability and the other test used to obtain the final measure (postmeasure) of algebra ability. The investigator then calculated a difference score (postmeasurement minus premeasurement) for each student, and computed the coefficient of correlation between these difference scores and initial scores. Inasmuch as the obtained coefficient of correlation was −0.4, the investigator concluded that the expected effect of the course has been realized.

(i) Use your knowledge of test theory to criticize this conclusion.

(ii) Describe how the experiment might have been conducted so as to avoid your criticism.

9.2. Calculate and interpret the coefficient of decision consistency and coefficient kappa for the results of a criterion-referenced testing experiment, reported in the following table:

		Second Test		Row
		Fail	Pass	Sums
First Test	Pass	15	47	62
	Fail	11	16	27
Column Sums		26	63	89

Notes

1. An alternative approach to defining the reliability of difference scores is through the coefficient of correlation between two parallel measures of change, say $D_{1p} = Y_{1p} - X_{1p}$ and $D_{2p} = Y_{2p} - X_{2p}$. This approach yields an expression identical to that given in Equation 9.6. Stanley (1967) derived a variant of Equation 9.6 for the situation involving second measures X_{2p} and Y_{2p}, which are *not* parallel to X_{1p} and Y_{1p}. This important development was used by Cronbach and Furby (1970) to define linked and unlinked measures or conditions of measurement, but we do not delve into this matter here.

2. In the present discussion, it is presumed there exist only two mastery states, say passing and failing. More than two mastery states have been considered in research by Huynh (1978) and Swaminathan, Hambleton, and Algina (1975), for example. These extensions, however, are not dealt with here.

10

An Evaluation of Classical Reliability Theory

Classical reliability theory is widely used for analyzing and interpreting educational measurements. Why should this be so? One reason is the intuitive appeal of the fundamental axiom of the theory, that an observed score is the sum of two constituent parts, a true score and an error score. As Lord (1959) observed, we find it easy to believe that measurements contain error, and if they do, there must be a complementary component in the measurement, which we have called true score. In addition to its intuitive appeal, the fundamental axiom of classical reliability theory is inherently weak in the sense that it cannot be proven false for a set of measurements. An observed score can always be viewed as the sum of a true score and an error score. So we can always accept the fundamental axiom of classical reliability theory, whereas the relatively stronger assumptions of theories that are, in principle at least, empirically testable may be unacceptable for given sets of test responses.

Going beyond the fundamental axiom of classical reliability theory, we have seen that if the concept of replicate measurements and the associated idea of the person-specific observed-score random variable are granted, then several basic results follow more or less directly. These results include the absence of correlation between the constituent true and error components of the observed measurements, and the concepts of standard error of measurement and reliability. Even when replicate measurements are not available and we cannot estimate directly, either the reliability of a set of measurements or the standard error of measurement for an examinee's observed score, we can often obtain approximate estimates or bounded estimates of these quantities.

Given the foregoing positive view of classical reliability theory, what arguments have been brought against it? Two main lines of criticism can be discerned in the literature on testing. The first is addressed to the meaning of measurement error, which, as we have seen, derives from the notion of replicate measurements. In imagination, the replicate measurements we make of some quality of a person are taken at the same time and in the same context as the measurement actually taken. These replicate measurements do not reflect variation due either to the time and place of the measurement or to the physical and psychological condition of the person being tested. They reflect only the variation in scores possible at the instant the test is given. Realists have difficulty making sense of this notion. They strive for operational meaning of the concept of replicate measurements by actually testing the person more than once with the same test on a different occasion, with a parallel form on a different occasion, or with comparable items within the same instrument. Each of these disparate notions of replication, as Guttman (1953) pointed out, lead to different conceptions of, and usually different numerical estimates of, the coefficient of reliability and the associated standard error of measurement. These different ways of conceptualizing replication and error of measurement prompted the development of generalizability theory (Brennan, 1983; Cronbach, Gleser, Nanda, & Rajaratnam, 1972; Shavelson & Webb, 1991), which provides a framework within which potential sources of extraneous variation in test scores can be identified, and the relative magnitudes of these sources of variation estimated. Countering the amorphous, but unitary, view of measurement error inherent in classical reliability theory is the view of generalizability theory that error of measurement is differentiated and multifaceted.

A second line of criticism of classical reliability theory has been enunciated by Hambleton and van der Linden (1982). These authors noted that, in the framework of classical reliability theory, (1) the score for a person is dependent on the test taken, and (2) the statistics for an item or a test are dependent on the sample of examinees tested. These points follow from the basic conception of true score, τ_p, as the expected value of the observed-score random variable, X_p. As should be clear from a reading of previous chapters, τ_p is unique to the combination of person *and* test. Moreover, statistics based on the distribution of scores for a collection of persons on a test are unique to the combination of test and the collection of persons tested. So, for example, the mean score for one test should be different from the mean score for another test of the same characteristic because the true scores on the first test will be different from those on the second test, regardless of how carefully the difficulty, discrimination, and score scales of the tests have been equated. Administer a more difficult test and a person's expected (true) score is likely to be lower, assuming a constant score scale. Administer a test to a more able group of examinees, and the mean of the distribution of raw scores on the test will increase, other factors remaining the same. What is desired is a theory or framework within which the measurement of a person and the test statistics for a group will be constant despite changes in the composition of the test. This notion has been captured by Wright (1968) in the evocative phrase "sample-free person measurement."

A branch of test theory referred to as item-response modeling can provide, under certain circumstances, the kind of sample-free measurement that is desired. The required circumstances are embodied in the assumptions of item-response models. A discussion of these assumptions would take us well beyond the scope of this volume. Those wishing to study item-response models can do so using another book in this series, by Hambleton et al. (1991). Suffice it to note that when the assumptions of item-response models are not satisfied in test data, the prudent course of action may be to work within the limitations of a weaker theory, one with assumptions almost certainly satisfied by test data of the kind usually collected. Classical reliability theory is a suitable choice under these circumstances.

Answers to Exercises

Chapter 1

1.1. Any number of different situations might be mentioned. For example, many different statistics could be drawn from the realm of sports, one being the percentage of greens a golfer achieves in the regulation number of strokes as a measure of golfing consistency or reliability. For a second example of a very different kind, consider a large metropolitan transportation system. The percentage of buses that return at the end of the day without having broken down is an indicator of the reliability of the fleet of vehicles. This index could be calculated every day for a period of time. Fluctuations in the index might signal improper maintenance or deterioration of the fleet.

Chapter 2

2.1. We are told that the possible outcomes of the coin toss are equally likely, which means we can assume $P_{Heads} = 0.5$ and $P_{Tails} = 0.5$. Applying Equation 2.1, we get the following result:

$$\mu = P_{Heads} \cdot 1 + P_{Tails} \cdot 2 = 0.5 \cdot 1 + 0.5 \cdot 2 = 0.5 + 1.0 = 1.5.$$

So the expected value of the specified random variable is 1.5.

2.2. To answer this question, we need to apply Equation 2.3, as follows:

$$\sigma^2 = P_{Heads}(1 - \mu)^2 + P_{Tails}(2 - \mu)^2 = 0.5(1 - 1.5)^2 + 0.5(2 - 1.5)^2$$

$$= 0.5(-0.5)^2 + 0.5(0.5)^2$$

$$= 0.25.$$

The variance of the random variable described in Question 2.1 is 0.25.

2.3. The calculations required to obtain the expected value and the variance of the IQ random variable described in Question 2.3 are indicated below:

IQ	P_x	$P_x x$	$x - \mu$	$(x - \mu)^2$	$P_x(x - \mu)^2$
70	0.0475	3.325	−30	900	42.75
80	0.1112	8.896	−20	400	44.48
90	0.2120	19.080	−10	100	21.20
100	0.2586	25.860	0	0	0.00
110	0.2120	23.320	10	100	21.20
120	0.1112	13.344	20	400	44.48
130	0.0475	6.175	30	900	42.75
	$\sum P_x$ $= 1.0000$	$\sum P_x x$ $= \varepsilon(X)$ $= 100$		$\sum P_x(x - \mu)^2 = \sigma_X^2$ $= 216.86$ $\sigma_x = 14.73$	

The expected value of the IQ random variable is 100, its variance is 216.86 (giving a standard deviation of 14.73).

2.4. To answer this question, we need to prepare the two-way table of joint probabilities and the associated marginal probabilities for the two random variables. This table is as follows:

		X 1	2	3	4	Margin
	4	0.00	0.00	0.05	0.10	0.15
	3	0.00	0.10	0.20	0.05	0.35
Y	2	0.05	0.20	0.10	0.00	0.35
	1	0.10	0.05	0.00	0.00	0.15
	Margin	0.15	0.35	0.35	0.15	1.00

The marginal probability distributions in this table can be used to compute the expected values and the variances of random variables X and Y. Using Equations 2.1 and 2.3, you can verify that $\mu_X = \mu_Y = 2.5$, and $\sigma_X^2 = \sigma_Y^2 = 0.85$.

The covariance between random variables X and Y is obtained using Equation 2.5 as follows:

$$\sigma_{XY} = \sum [P_{xy}(x - \mu_X)(y - \mu_y)]$$

$$= 0.00(4 - 2.5)(1 - 2.5) + 0.00(4 - 2.5)(2 - 2.5)$$

$$+ 0.05(4 - 2.5)(3 - 2.5) + 0.10(4 - 2.5)(4 - 2.5) + \ldots$$

$$+ 0.10(1 - 2.5)(1 - 2.5) + 0.05(1 - 2.5)(2 - 2.5)$$

$$+ 0.00(1 - 2.5)(3 - 2.5) + 0.00(1 - 2.5)(4 - 2.5)$$

$$= 0.65$$

So, the covariance of random variables X and Y is 0.65.

Using Equation 2.7 and the covariance and variances of random variables X and Y, we can calculate the coefficient of correlation between the variables as follows:

$$\rho_{XY} = \frac{\sigma_{XY}}{\sigma_X \sigma_Y} = \frac{0.65}{\sqrt{0.85}\sqrt{0.85}} = \frac{0.65}{0.85} = 0.76.$$

Chapter 3

3.1. Given the scoring rule in effect for the test, observed scores must be whole numbers, ranging from 0 to 10, inclusive. Thus, of the four numbers 8, 3.6, 10, and 1.111, only 8 and 10 are possible observed scores. Because true scores have been presented as expected values (means) of person-specific observed-score random variables, each of the four numbers is a possible true score. If 10 were a true score, however, the associated observed-score random variable could only yield scores of 10, so the PSEM for this true score would be 0.

Error scores are obtained by subtracting true from observed scores, so this might suggest that all four scores are potential error scores. But only the scores 8, 3.6, and 1.111 could possibly be error scores. The reason 10 cannot be an error score is that an error score of this magnitude could arise for this test only if the observed score were 10 and the true score were 0. This result is logically impossible. A person with a true score of 0 should obtain observed scores of only 0, and 10 is a logically impossible observed score. This discussion rests on the presupposition that observed scores greater than 0 cannot be achieved by chance, as in guessing answers to multiple-choice test items. If scores greater than 0 can be attained by chance, then the true score, as the expected value of the observed-score random variable, would necessarily be greater than 0, in which case 10 could not be an error score, although an observed score of 10 would be possible.

3.2. To begin, consider what a Platonic true score is not: It is not the expected value of a random variable. Instead, it is a number that applies to a characteristic of the individual, regardless of the number obtained in an attempt to measure the characteristic. For example, the number of siblings a person has is a characteristic for which there is a Platonic true score. We might measure this characteristic in a variety of ways—ask the person, ask a relative, search the birth records of the communities in which the family lived, and so forth. Not all of these ways of measuring the characteristic will necessarily give the same answer. Nevertheless, the person has exactly a given number of siblings, and this number is not necessarily equal to the average of all the different measurements that might be made of the characteristic.

3.3. (i) $\sigma_T^2 \leq \sigma_X^2$

(ii) Given no information about σ_X^2, it is not possible to define a relationship between the magnitudes of σ_T^2 and σ_E^2. Given σ_X^2, we can write the strict equality, $\sigma_E^2 = \sigma_X^2 - \sigma_T^2$.

3.4. What is described in this question are the estimates of the probability distributions of essay ratings for the two examinees. The distribution for the first examinee does not overlap the distribution of the second examinee. Clearly, the true score of the first examinee—the expected value of his or her probability distribution—is less than that of the second examinee. The PSEM of the first examinee, however, is less than the PSEM of the second examinee.

Chapter 4

4.1. $\rho_X^2 = \dfrac{\sigma_T^2}{\sigma_X^2} = \dfrac{190}{225} = 0.84$ (approximately).

4.2. $\rho_X^2 = \dfrac{\sigma_T^2}{\sigma_X^2} = \dfrac{\sigma_X^2 - \sigma_E^2}{\sigma_X^2} = 1 - \dfrac{\sigma_E^2}{\sigma_X^2} = 1 - \dfrac{SEM^2}{\sigma_X^2}$

$= 1 - \dfrac{4.5^2}{10^2} = 1 - \dfrac{20.25}{100} = 1 - 0.2025 = 0.80$ (approximately).

4.3. For observations on a person-specific observed-score random variable X_p, we can write the statement

$$\text{Prob}(\tau_p - \sigma_{E_p} \leq X_p \leq \tau_p + \sigma_{E_p}) = 0.68,$$

which probability holds provided X_p is approximately normally distributed. Manipulating terms, this expression translates into a confidence interval for τ_p, when $X_p = 85$ and $\sigma_{E_p} = 5$, of $[85 - 5, 85 + 5]$ or $[80, 90]$.

4.4. Given an observed score of 97 and a SEM of 5, the 68% confidence interval would be [92, 102]. But, because the maximum possible test score is 100, true scores greater than 100 are impossible. This implies that either the PSEM for the examinee who achieves a score of 97 is less than 5, or the observed score of 97 is unusually large for the observed-score random variable X_p. These implications are not mutually exclusive, so both could be correct.

Chapter 5

5.1. The observed-score random variables for parallel tests should have equal expected values (means) and equal standard deviations. So, the observed-score random variable for the parallel test must have an expected value of 100 and a standard deviation of 15.

5.2. $\sigma_E^2 = \sigma_X^2(1 - \rho_X^2) = 400(1 - 0.92) = 400(0.08) = 32.$

5.3. —[1]. $\sigma_{12} = 42$. This result follows from a basic expression for the coefficient of correlation, that is,

$$\rho_{12} = \frac{\sigma_{12}}{\sigma_1\sigma_2},$$

because only the term σ_{12} of this expression is not given in the table ($\rho_{12} = 0.75$, $\sigma_1 = 7$, and $\sigma_2 = 8$).

—[2]. $\rho_{23} = 0.79$ (rounded to two decimal places). This result follows directly once we have a value for σ_3, the answer for the third blank.

—[3]. The value of σ_3 is approximately 10. This value can be obtained by (1) writing the expression for ρ_{23}, that is, the analogue of that given in the answer for —[1], (2) seeing that the covariance and coefficient of correlation for Tests 1 and 3 and the standard deviation of Test 1 are given, (3) substituting them in the expression for the coefficient of correlation [that is, $\rho_{13} = \sigma_{13}/\sigma_1\sigma_3$], and (4) solving for the unknown value of σ_3. A second estimate of σ_3 could be obtained in similar fashion, using the information available for Tests 3 and 4.

—[4]. The value of this mean cannot be determined from the information given. The congeneric model imposes no constraints on the test means. The focus in congeneric models is on variances and covariances, hence also on coefficients of correlation.

Chapter 6

6.1. The assumption of independence of measurements has been violated. One expects the coefficient of correlation between the ratings of independent judges to be less than 1.

6.2. (i) Inasmuch as parallel forms are being used, and such forms are composed of different questions, we expect question-by-examinee interaction to contribute to measurement error. In addition, the interaction due to occasion-by-examinee interaction would contribute to measurement error. This latter interaction could be caused by differential examinee reactions to whatever differences there were in the conditions under which the tests were administered on the two occasions, or to differential changes in examinee ability.

(ii) The correlation would be expected to be less than 0.78. The greater the length of time between test administrations, the more examinees can be expected to change differentially, with these changes increasing the amount of occasion-by-examinee interaction variance, which variance, in this context, adds to error variance.

6.3. It is proven in Sidebar 6.4 that the Rulon formula (Equation 6.3) returns a result equal to the reliability of the full-length test provided (i) the correlation between true scores on the two half-tests is equal to 1, and (ii) the standard deviation of the true-score distributions on both half-tests are equal. These conditions are satisfied for parallel tests, and for so-called tau-equivalent and essentially tau-equivalent tests. When the aforementioned two requirements are not satisfied, the Rulon formula returns a number that can be interpreted as a lower bound to reliability.

6.4. Using formulas given in Chapter 6:

$$L_1 = 1 - \frac{18.6}{54} = 0.66.$$

$$L_3 = \alpha = \frac{4}{3}L_1 = 0.87.$$

$$L_2 = L_1 + \left(\frac{4}{3}\right)\frac{\sqrt{112.1}}{54} = 0.92.$$

Chapter 7

7.1. This question calls for application of the generalized Spearman-Brown formula (Equation 7.1). The answers are 0.75 for a test double the length of the original test, 0.82 for a test of triple length, and 0.43 for a test one-half the length of the original.

7.2. (i) Regardless of the index of item quality that is selected—the item-total correlation coefficient or the index of reliability—the two worst performing items are numbered 7 and 11.

(ii) Using the item-total correlation, the four strongest items are numbered 2, 4, 5, and 6. Using the index of reliability, the strongest are items those numbered 4, 5, 6, and 8. Items 2 and 8 have very nearly the same item-total correlation coefficient—0.49 versus 0.48. But Item 8, with the smaller item-total correlation coefficient, has a much larger standard deviation than Item 2—0.49 versus 0.41. So Item 8 also has a much larger index of reliability than Item 2.

Chapter 8

8.1. According to a result developed in Sidebar 8.1, an unbiased estimate of the variance of the person-specific error random variable for parallel half-tests for an examinee is given by the squared difference between scores on the two half-tests. Thus the estimate of error variance is $\hat{\sigma}_E^2 = (10 - 13)^2 = 9$. The estimated PSEM for this examinee is 3, the square root of 9.

8.2. (i) To apply equation 4.2.3, we require estimates of σ_X and ρ_X^2. The former quantity is the sum of the indices of reliability for the items in a test. This sum for the Mathematics Test, according to Table 7.1, is 5.01. Coefficient KR_{20} (Equation 6.3) can be used as an estimate of the reliability coefficient ρ_X^2. To apply Equation 6.3, we need (1) an estimate of the variance of the observed-score random variable for the total test, $\sigma_X^2 (= 5.01^2 = 25.10)$ and (2) the sum of the variances of the observed-score random variables for the items in the test (given in Table 7.1 as 7.03). Substituting accordingly in Equation 6.3, we get $\hat{\rho}_X^2 = KR_{20} = 0.74$. Finally, substituting in Equation 4.2.3, we obtain 2.55 as the estimate (to two decimal places) of the average SEM for the Mathematics Test.

(ii) The average SEM of 2.55 is a little larger than the estimated PSEMs for scores at the extremes of the score scale for the total test, and a little smaller than the estimated PSEMs for scores on the total test in the range 19 to 23 (see Table 8.1). Using the average SEM, the length of a 68% confidence interval for a true score on the test would be 5.1. The length of 68% confidence intervals based on estimated PSEMs will range from 4.8 to 5.4, depending on total test score. The maximum difference in length of 68% confidence intervals between those based on PSEMs and those based on the average SEM is seen to be on the order of ±5%.

Chapter 9

9.1. (i) We know from the analysis presented in Sidebar 9.1 that error of measurement in the premeasure (say E_X) is negatively correlated with the difference between the errors of measurement in the pre- and postmeasures (say $E_Y - E_X$). This difference in measurement error is present in the difference score (say $X - Y$) that is obtained by subtracting the premeasure of algebra ability from the postmeasure of algebra ability. Consequently, the negative correlation observed in the experiment is at least partially spurious, due to the fact that error of measurement for the premeasure is present in both of the variables being correlated, but with opposite signs. In the light of this argument, the observed correlation, −0.4, is larger in absolute value than it would be, had the errors of measurement on the premeasure been independent of the errors of measurement in the difference scores.

(ii) The ideal strategy for avoiding correlated errors of measurement in the situation described in this question is to develop three parallel forms of the test of algebra ability. Two of these tests can be administered as premeasures and the third can be used as the postmeasure. The errors of measurement in each test can be expected to be statistically independent of, hence uncorrelated with, the errors of measurement on either of the other tests. If one premeasure is then combined with the postmeasure for the purpose of calculating difference scores, and the other premeasure is correlated with this difference-score variable, the result should be a coefficient of correlation that is free of the effect of any spurious negative correlation between errors of measurement.

9.2. The estimated coefficient of decision consistency for these data is $\hat{\pi}_{dc} =$ $(47 + 11)/89 = 0.65$. This coefficient is interpreted to mean that approximately 65% of examinees in the population would be similarly classified, either as passing or as failing, on repeated testing.

To obtain an estimate of κ, we need the following intermediate result:

$$\hat{\pi}_c = \left(\frac{62}{89}\right)\left(\frac{63}{89}\right) + \left(\frac{27}{89}\right)\left(\frac{26}{89}\right) = 0.58 .$$

This statistic is the expected proportion of persons who, on repeated testing, would be similarly classified by chance (as passing or as failing), assuming the marginal frequencies of the table of results given in the question are fixed.

Thus, the estimate of κ_{dc} is as follows:

$$\hat{\kappa}_{dc} = \frac{0.65 - 0.58}{1.00 - 0.58} = 0.17 .$$

References

Algina, J., & Noe, M. J. (1978). A study of the accuracy of Subkoviak's single-administration estimate of the coefficient of agreement using two true-score estimates. *Journal of Educational Measurement, 15,* 101-110.

Angoff, W. H. (1971). Scales, norms, and equivalent scores. In R. L. Thorndike (Ed.), *Educational measurement* (2nd ed., pp. 508-600). Washington, DC: American Council on Education.

Brennan, R. L. (1983). *Elements of generalizability theory.* Iowa City, IA: ACT Publications.

Brown, W. (1910). Some experimental results in the correlation of mental abilities. *British Journal of Psychology, 3,* 296-322.

Committee of AERA, APA, & NCME. (1985). *Standards for educational and psychological testing.* Washington, DC: American Psychological Association.

Crocker, L., & Algina, J. (1986). *Introduction to classical and modern test theory.* New York: Holt, Rinehart and Winston.

Cronbach, L. J. (1951). Coefficient alpha and the internal structure of tests. *Psychometrika, 16,* 297-334.

Cronbach, L. J., & Furby, L. (1970). How should we measure "change"—or should we? *Psychological Bulletin, 74,* 68-80.

Cronbach, L. J., Gleser, G. C., Nanda, H., & Rajaratnam, N. (1972). *The dependability of behavioral measurements: Theory of generalizability for scores and profiles.* New York: John Wiley.

de Gruijter, D. N. M., & van der Kamp, L. J. Th. (1984). *Statistical models in psychological and educational testing.* Lisse: Swets & Zeitlinger.

Feldt, L. S., & Brennan, R. L. (1989). Reliability. In R. L. Linn (Ed.), *Educational measurement* (3rd ed., pp. 105-146). New York: Macmillan.

Fleishman, J., & Benson, J. (1987). Using LISREL to evaluate measurement models and scale reliability. *Educational and Psychological Measurement, 47,* 925-939.

Gulliksen, H. (1950). *Theory of mental tests.* New York: John Wiley.

Guttman, L. (1945). A basis for analyzing test-retest reliability. *Psychometrika, 10,* 255-282.

Guttman, L. (1953). A special review of Harold Gulliksen, *Theory of mental tests. Psychometrika, 18,* 123-130.

Hambleton, R. K., & Novick, M. R. (1973). Toward an integration of theory and method for criterion-referenced tests. *Journal of Educational Measurement, 10,* 159-170.

Hambleton, R. K., Swaminathan, H., & Rogers, H. J. (1991). *Fundamentals of item response theory*. Newbury Park, CA: Sage.

Hambleton, R. K., & van der Linden, W. J. (1982). Advances in item response theory and applications: An introduction. *Applied Psychological Measurement, 6,* 373-378.

Huynh, H. (1976). On the reliability of decisions in domain-referenced testing. *Journal of Educational Measurement, 13,* 253-264.

Huynh, H. (1978). Reliability of multiple classifications. *Psychometrika, 43,* 317-325.

Jones, L. V. (1971). The nature of measurement. In R. L. Thorndike (Ed.), *Educational measurement* (2nd ed., pp. 335-355). Washington, DC: American Council on Education.

Jöreskog, K. G., & Sörbom, D. (1989). *LISREL 7 user's reference guide*. Mooresville, IL: Scientific Software.

Keeping, E. S. (1962). *Introduction to statistical inference*. Princeton, NJ: Van Nostrand.

Kuder, G. F., & Richardson, M. W. (1937). The theory of the estimation of test reliability. *Psychometrika, 2,* 151-160.

Linn, R. L., & Werts, C. E. (1979). Covariance structures and their analysis. In R. E. Traub (Ed.), *New directions for testing and measurement: Methodological developments* (No. 4, pp. 53-73). San Francisco: Jossey-Bass.

Lord, F. M. (1956). The measurement of growth. *Educational and Psychological Measurement, 16,* 421-437.

Lord, F. M. (1958). Further problems in the measurement of growth. *Educational and Psychological Measurement, 18,* 437-454.

Lord, F. M. (1959). An approach to mental test theory. *Psychometrika, 24,* 283-302.

Lord, F. M. (1963). Elementary models for measuring change. In C. W. Harris (Ed.), *Problems in measuring change*. Madison: University of Wisconsin Press.

Lord, F. M., & Novick, M. R. (1968). *Statistical theories of mental test scores*. Reading, MA: Addison-Wesley.

Manning, W. H., & DuBois, P. H. (1962). Correlational methods in research on human learning. *Perceptual and Motor Skills, 15,* 287-321.

Marascuilo, L. A., & Serlin, R. C. (1988). *Statistical methods for the social and behavioral sciences*. New York: Freeman.

Merriam-Webster's Collegiate Dictionary (10th ed.). (1993). Springfield, MA: Merriam-Webster.

Millman, J. (1979). Reliability and validity of criterion-referenced test scores. In R. Traub (Ed.), *New directions for testing and measurement: Methodological developments* (No. 4, pp. 75-92). San Francisco: Jossey-Bass.

MINITAB, Inc. (1989). *MINITAB statistical software* (Release 7). State College, PA: Author.

Novick, M. R. (1966). The axioms and principal results of classical test theory. *Journal of Mathematical Psychology, 3,* 1-18.

Novick, M. R., & Lewis, C. (1967). Coefficient alpha and the reliability of composite measurements. *Psychometrika, 32,* 1-13.

Popham, W. J., & Husek, T. R. (1969). Implications of criterion-referenced measurement. *Journal of Educational Measurement, 6,* 1-9.

Rogosa, D. R., Brandt, D., & Zimowski, M. (1982). A growth curve approach to the measurement of change. *Psychological Bulletin, 90,* 726-748.

Rogosa, D. R., Floden, R., & Willett, J. B. (1984). Assessing the stability of teacher behavior. *Journal of Educational Psychology, 76,* 1000-1027.

Rogosa, D. R., & Willett, J. B. (1983). Demonstrating the reliability of the difference score in the measurement of change. *Journal of Educational Measurement, 20,* 335-343.

Rogosa, D. R., & Willett, J. B. (1985). Understanding correlates of change by modeling individual differences in growth. *Psychometrika, 50,* 203-228.

Rulon, P. J. (1939). A simplified procedure for determining the reliability of a test by split halves. *Harvard Educational Review, 9,* 99-103.

Shavelson, R. J., & Webb, N. M. (1991). *Generalizability theory: A primer.* Newbury Park, CA: Sage.

Spearman, C. (1904). The proof and measurement of association between two things. *American Journal of Psychology, 15,* 72-101.

Spearman, C. (1907). Demonstration of formulae for true measurement of correlation. *American Journal of Psychology, 18,* 161-169.

Spearman, C. (1910). Correlation calculated from faulty data. *British Journal of Psychology, 3,* 271-295.

Spray, J. A., & Welch, C. J. (1990). Estimation of classification consistency when the probability of a correct response varies. *Journal of Educational Measurement, 27,* 15-25.

Stanley, J. C. (1967). General and special formulas for reliability of differences. *Journal of Educational Measurement, 4,* 249-252.

Stevens, S. S. (1948). Mathematics, measurement, and psychophysics. In S. S. Stevens (Ed.), *Handbook of experimental psychology* (pp. 1-49). New York: John Wiley.

Subkoviak, M. J. (1976). Estimating reliability from a single administration of a criterion-referenced test. *Journal of Educational Measurement, 13,* 265-276.

Subkoviak, M. J. (1978). Empirical investigation of procedures for estimating reliability for mastery tests. *Journal of Educational Measurement, 15,* 111-116.

Swaminathan, H., Hambleton, R. K., & Algina, J. (1974). Reliability of criterion-referenced tests: A decision-theoretic formulation. *Journal of Educational Measurement, 11,* 263-267.

Swaminathan, H., Hambleton, R. K., & Algina, J. (1975). A Bayesian decision-theoretic procedure for use with criterion-referenced tests. *Journal of Educational Measurement, 12,* 87-98.

Traub, R. E., & Rowley, G. L. (1980). Reliability of test scores and decisions. *Applied Psychological Measurement, 4,* 517-545.

Tucker, L. J., Damarin, F., & Messick, S. (1966). A base-free measure of change. *Psychometrika, 31,* 457-473.

Willett, J. B. (1988-1989). Questions and answers in the measurement of change. In E. Z. Rothkopf (Ed.), *Review of research in education* (Vol. 15, pp. 345-422). Washington, DC: American Educational Research Association.

Woodruff, D. (1990). Conditional standard error of measurement in prediction. *Journal of Educational Measurement, 27,* 191-208.

Wright, B. D. (1968). Sample-free test calibration and person measurement. *Proceedings of the 1967 Invitational Conference on Testing Problems.* Princeton, NJ: Educational Testing Service.

Author Index

Algina, J., 141, 143, 151, 153
Angoff, W. H., 134

Benson, J., 54
Brandt, D., 137
Brennan, R. L., xi, 97, 155
Brown, W., 79

Committee of AERA, APA, NCME, 115
Cronbach, L. J., 83, 86, 135, 136, 153, 155

Damarin, F., 135
DuBois, P. H., 135

Feldt, L. S., xi, 97
Fleishman, J., 54
Floden, R., 137
Furby, L., 135, 136, 153

Gleser, G. C., 155
Guttman, L., 83, 87, 91, 155

Hambleton, R. K., 3, 141, 143, 153, 155, 156
Husek, T. R., 139
Huynh, H., 151, 153

Jones, L. V., 2
Jöreskog, K. G., 54, 59

Keeping, E. S., 11
Kuder, G. F., 82

Lewis, C., 86
Linn, R. L., 54
Lord, F. M., xi, 1, 22, 74, 79, 113, 135, 154

Manning, W. H., 135
Marascuilo, L. A., 16, 42
Messick, S., 135
Millman, J., 146
MINITAB, Inc., 74

Nanda, H., 155
Noe, M. J., 151
Novick, M. R., xi, 1, 22, 74, 79, 86, 113, 141

Popham, W. J., 139

Rajaratnam, N., 155
Richardson, M. W., 82-83
Rogers, H. J., 3, 156
Rogosa, D. R., 137
Rowley, G. L., 141, 145, 151

168

Rulon, P. J., 80

Serlin, R. C., 16, 42
Shavelson, R. J., ix, 3, 62, 110, 155
Sörbom, D., 54, 60
Spearman, C., 1, 79
Spray, J. A., 151
Stanley, J. C., 153
Stevens, S. S., 2
Subkoviak, M. J., 146, 148, 151, 152
Swaminathan, H., 3, 141, 143, 153, 156

Traub, R. E., 141, 145, 151

Tucker, L. J., 135

van der Linden, W. J., 155

Webb, N. M., ix, 3, 62, 110, 155
Welch, C. J., 151
Werts, C. E., 54
Willett, J. B., 137, 138
Woodruff, D., 120, 123
Wright, B. D., 156

Zimowski, M., 137

Subject Index

ANOVA:
   reliability estimation calculation and, 73-75

Biserial coefficient, 112, 113

Coefficient of correlation:
   between two random variables, 15-16, 49
Coefficient of decision consistency, 141-142
Coefficient of reliability, 110
   proof concerning coefficient of
      correlation as estimator of, 76-77
Congeneric test hypothesis, 57-59, 62, 64, 70
   basic assumptions underlying, 57-59
   implications of, 59
   proofs of several results for, 60-61

Decision consistency:
   calculating indices of, 144
   deciding which indices of to use, 145-146
   demonstration of application of
      Subkoviak index to, 149
   Huynh's estimate of, 151
   implementing Subkoviak's index of, 150, 152
   indexing of, 141
   single-administration estimates of, 146-151

Subkoviak index of, 146-149, 151

Error of measurement, 18, 24-25
   classical reliability theory and, 155
   definition of, 19, 24
   properties of random variable for, 25
Error score, 18, 36
   definition of, 19
   variance in, 24-25
   See also Error of measurement
Essentially Tau-equivalent tests,
      hypothesis of, 56-57, 59, 62, 63, 70

Flanagan, J., 80

Generalizability theory, 3, 62, 110, 155

Item response modeling, 156
Item response theory, 3

Kuder–Richardson formula 20
   and coefficient alpha, 82-83, 86-87

Measurement:
   concept of, 1-3
   criterion-referenced approach to, 139
   definition of , 1-2
   implications of conception of, 30-33

mental versus physical, 138
normed-reference approach to, 138
on interval scales, 2, 3
on ratio scales, 2, 3
purpose of, 138
quality used in social science research
and applications, 3
Measurement, criterion-referenced
approach to, 139, 140, 151-152
decision consistency and, 141
example of, 140
issue of variance and, 140
Measurement, normed-reference
approach to, 138
reliability in context of, 139
Measurement error. *See* Error of
measurement; Error score
Measurement growth/change:
concomitant measures and, 135
demonstration that correlated errors of
measurement can bias the
prediction of, 132
differences in means and issue of
reliability and, 129-130
estimated true change and, 135
fundamental difficulties in, 130-131
importance of in social science
research, 136-137
linear regression and, 135
longitudinal approach to, 137-138
predicting, 131-133
profile chart/graph and, 133-134
reliability of difference scores and,
126-138
residual change scores and, 135
SEM for difference scores and,
134-135
simple difference scores and,
127-129, 135
studying profiles and, 133-134
true residual change and, 135
Measurement sets:
estimating reliability of, 4
Measuring:
describing process of, 2
more than one person, 28-34
MINITAB, 74

Nesting, definition of, 59

Observed measurements/scores, 18, 36
distribution of, 28
sources of variation of, 30
viewed as sum of true score and error
score, 29

Parallel tests, 4, 62, 63, 70, 136
and estimating the SEM, 53
and reliability coefficient estimation,
46-50
assumptions and consequences
pertaining to covariances of, 50-51
characteristics of assumptions for,
47-49
definition of, 47
importance of, 50, 53
testing the hypothesis of, 53-62
Parallel tests, hypothesis of, 62, 64
alternatives to, 54-59
Pearson product-moment coefficient of
correlation, 15, 76-77, 109, 112
Person-specific observed-score random
variables, 46
Person-specific random variable, 20, 21,
31
Person-specific standard error of
measurement (PSEM), 26, 114,
115, 121
demonstration that grouping
examinees by total test scores gives
biased estimates of, 122-123
proof that squared difference between
parallel part-test scores estimates,
118-119
Platonic true score, 20-21
extended discussion of, 22
Point-biserial coefficient, 112-113
Probability density, 11

Random variable, 3, 5, 6-7
definition of, 6, 16
Random variable, continuous, 16

Random variable, discrete, 10, 16
Random variable, expected value of, 3,
     5, 7-11
     redefining true score as, 19
     versus arithmetic mean, 7
Random variable, moments of, 11
Random variable, observation of:
     error score and, 19
     true score and, 19
Random variable, variance of, 5, 11-12
     and moments referred to the mean, 11
     a proof of the equality of two
         expressions for, 13
Random variables:
     coefficient of correlation between
         two, 15-16
     relationships among, 36
     types of, 36
Random variables, covariance of two, 5,
     12-15
Reliability, 38-45
     ANOVA estimate of, 79
     as correlation coefficient, 50-53
     correlation estimate of, 79
     decision consistency as, 140-141
     history of concept of, 1
     lower bounds to, 87-89, 94
Reliability, special topics involving,
     126-153
     criterion-referenced measurement,
         126, 138-151
     measurement of growth or change,
         126-138
Reliability coefficient, 4, 38-39, 44
     and obtaining estimate of SEM, 39
     explanation of symbol for, 40
     uses of, 39-44
Reliability coefficient, factors affecting,
     98-113
     heterogeneity of population of
         examinees, 110
     item characteristics, 101-109
     quality of scoring of subjectively
         scored items, 109-110
     test length, 99-101, 111
     time limits, 98-99, 110-111
Reliability coefficient estimation, 46-65
     experiments and formulas, 66-97

Reliability estimation by testing more
     than once, 70-75
     alternate-forms estimate of reliability,
         70, 72-73, 94
     test-retest coefficient of reliability
         and, 70, 71-72, 94
Reliability estimation by testing only
     once, 75-94
     sources of extraneous variance in
         estimates of SEM from, 75-77
Reliability estimation calculation, 73-75,
     77-79
Reliability experiments:
     experimental independence of
         measurements in, 67-69, 94
     factors to consider in conducting,
         66-70
     identical administrative procedures for
         the experiment and subsequent
         applications, 67, 69, 94
     sample representativeness in, 67, 94
     sample size in, 67
     two or more measurements in, 67,
         69-70, 94
Reliability theory:
     basic, 18-37
     definition of, xi
     derivation of, 18
     for criterion-referenced
         measurements, 138-151
     introduction of formal statement of, 1
     measurement limitations and, 2-3
     models for, 63-64
     published accounts of, xi
     See also Reliability theory, classical
Reliability theory, classical, 116
     alternatives to, 3
     and identifying flaws in measuring
         process, 3
     arguments against, 154-156
     as based on weak assumptions, 33
     basic tenants of, 4
     evaluation of, 154-156
     fundamental equation of, 19
     reasons for use in analyzing and
         interpreting educational
         measurements, 154
     results of, 34

See also Reliability theory
Repeated measurement experiment, 18-28
Rulon formula, 95
   and lower bound to test reliability, 81, 96
   and nonparallel test components, 80-81
   derivation of, 84-85

Sample-free person measurement, 156
Spearman-Brown formula, 78, 79-80, 95,
      98, 99
   derivation of, 82-83
Spearman-Brown formula, generalized,
      100, 101, 111
Speeded tests, 98
   and reliability of test sores, 98-99
Standard error of measurement (SEM),
      25-28, 46, 114
   parallel tests as means of estimating, 53
   some theory for, 115-118
Standard error of measurement (SEM)
      estimation, 4, 41, 44, 114-125
   practical but flawed approach to,
      118-120
   Woodruff approach to, 120-121, 124

Tau-equivalent tests, hypothesis of,
      54-56, 59, 61-62, 63, 70
Test item characteristics, reliability of
      scores and, 101-109
   heterogeneity of examinee population,
      110, 111

index of difficulty and, 108-109, 111
index of discrimination and, 101,
      107-108, 111
index of reliability and, 101, 104-107,
      111
item validity and, 107
subjectively scored test items and
      quality of scoring and, 109-110,
      111
test composition and examinee
      sample, 107
Test length, 99-101
   demonstration of effect of doubling on
      variances of true and error scores,
      102-103
   Spearman-Brown formula and,
      100-101
Test scores, 6
True score, 18, 20-23, 36, 46
   definition of, 21
   obtaining confidence interval for 42,
      114
   redefinition of, 19
   sources of variation of, 30
   variation in, 29-30, 34-35
True score regression estimates:
   problems with, 150-151

Variable, 5-6
   definition of, 5
Variables, categorical:
   examples of, 6

About the Author

Ross E. Traub is Professor of Education at the Ontario Institute for Studies in Education, where he teaches graduate courses in psychometrics, educational measurement, and statistics. His university education was obtained from the University of Alberta (B.Ed., M.Ed.) and Princeton University (Ph.D., Psychology). While attending Princeton University, he held a Psychometric Fellowship from the Educational Testing Service, and first engaged test theory seriously under the tutelage of Frederick M. Lord. His research interests range from test theory in particular to psychometrics in general, and from the effects of item format on test performance in particular to the enterprises of large-scale educational assessment in general, with these interests reflected in more than 40 refereed publications. He served a term as Editor of *Journal of Educational Measurement,* is currently serving as an Associate Editor of *Journal of Educational Statistics* and *Psychometrika,* and is also a member of the Editorial Boards of *Applied Measurement in Education* and *Applied Psychological Measurement.* He is Past-President of the Canadian Educational Researchers Association, and has been an active member of the American Educational Research Association and the National Council on Measurement in Education.